Untying Aristotle: Poetics for Storytellers

Rune Myrland

Storyknot * August 8, 2020

First edition, March 2018

ISBN: 978-19-8059-153-5

www.storyknot.com
editorial@storyknot.com

Special thanks to Josefine Kjærstad, Robert Emil Berge and Bernt Kenneth Robstad for reading drafts and offering valuable feedback. They have saved me from embarrassing mistakes. Those left are my own. Also to Øivind Andersen for responding to questions and offering encouragement and to Arbogast Schmitt for discussion.

Contents

Aristotle's Poetics   **60**

Cited Sources   **119**

The Cast (in Order of Appearance)

The Wandering Bard

Nine years have passed since the Trojan War ended, and Odysseus has not yet shown up. Most think he is dead. 108 suitors are abusing the hospitality of his manor and demanding that his wife Penelope chooses one of them as her new husband. She delays the decision. Meanwhile, the suitors spend their days feasting, butchering the livestock and eating the hosts to poverty. This is their right, they say, as long as Penelope cannot make up her mind.

The *Odyssey* is about twelve thousand lines of hexameter verse, eight times the length of a Greek tragedy. It tells the story about the difficult homecoming from the Trojan War for the hero Odysseus.

The plot does not begin in Troy where the journey begins. It begins nine years later at Ithaca, his home, showing it in a state where his return is urgently needed. This is not the chronological beginning. It is what Aristotle calls the beginning of a whole action. Homer starts the *Odyssey* by setting up the problem that will be solved in the ending.

Stephen Tracy (1997) has noted that Homer often uses ring composition. When Odysseus meets his mother in the underworld, he asks her a number of questions. She replies to them in opposite order. The last first.

Homer does not stop at using ring composition in dialogue. The whole poem is composed in this manner. Instead of creating an episodic structure by giving the characters a series of problems, each solved in turn, he stacks them up. First he poses one problem, then a second, then a third, then a fourth.

When the stack is tall enough, he takes a problem or three off, the last one first. Then he can add a few again, and then he removes a few. But he never removes the one posed in the beginning until the ending. This gives unity to the plot.

Why compose a poem that takes several days to recite in this way?

We do not know. We know very little about Homer. Much of what has been suggested is based on the blind bard Demodocus in the *Odyssey*. What we have is the *Homeric Question*, which is really a number of questions. Was the *Iliad* and *Odyssey* composed by one, two, or many poets? What role, if any, did writing play in their composition? It has been proven that the poems are indebted to an oral tradition and that some passages are very old, but that is about it.

I imagine Homer as a bard traveling from place to place. In the evenings he plays the lyre and sings his narrative poem in exchange for hospitality and food. He stays in each place a few days before he moves on.

To create an artistic unity or to secure hospitality for a little longer, he sets up a problem on the first night that will be resolved in the last. But he also has a few that are resolved the same night.

However it came to be, Homer's way of plotting has come down to us as our way.

The Tragedy Competitions

Three hundred or so years after Homer, in a culture that has canonized the *Iliad* and the *Odyssey*, we find the ancient Greek tragedy competitions. They were held during the big City Dionysia in Athens, in front of up to 15,000 spectators. It is, in more ways than one would imagine, the cradle of modern storytelling.

The Dionysia were festivals held in honor of Dionysus, the god of the grape harvest and wine-making. As one might expect, these were big parties with ritualistic drinking, singing, and dancing. Live entertainment was the thing in those days, as it was the only option. Recording technologies would not be invented for another couple of millennia, unless you count writing, which, let's be honest, does not lend itself to partying.

There were two Dionysia, the small Rural Dionysia held in winter and the huge City Dionysia in Athens held during spring. One can imagine the festival crowd of the day wanting a taste of both.

The tragedy may have evolved from the dithyramb, a ritualistic song and dance number performed in honor of Dionysus. During the sixth century BCE, the shining star on the dithyramb sky was the singer Thespis, who is often credited with inventing both acting and the tragedy. He is known for putting his show on the road, and it is said he invented theatrical touring as well.

The word tragedy means goat song. The genre may have gotten its name from the first prize in early competitions. The first one we know of was won by Thespis at the City Dionysia in Athens in 534 BCE.

During the following centuries, these tragedy competitions were the big thing in ancient Greek entertainment, second only to athletic competitions. In time there were comedy competitions as well, but if Aristotle is to be trusted, it took a while for the genre to be taken seriously (Poetics 5/49b1).

The three competition playwrights were selected half a year ahead. In a measure to cut on public spending, they were assigned private sponsors who would pay for much of the production cost. Customarily each playwright took part with three tragedies and one satyr play, which were shown to the festival crowd during a three-day binge-watching marathon.

The best playwright was chosen by a secret jury. Formally the winner was the man who sponsored him, but of course the playwright won as well.

The tragedy competitions were an ideal arena for testing ideas and learning what worked with the audience or not. During the first hundred or so years, the principles for evoking suspense and empathy were found and refined to the level that is still practiced today. The evolution of the genre was spearheaded by stars like Aeschylus (winner in 472, 467, 463 and 458 BCE), Euripides (winner in 441, 428 and 405 BCE) and Sophocles (winner in 468, 447, 438, 409 and 401 BCE), who we still have plays by.

On average the names of fifty playwrights are known from each century. Nine tragedies, five comedies and three satyr plays were shown in a normal year, which means about 1700 original plays were written for the City Dionysia per century.

Thus, when Aristotle (384 – 322 BCE) came around to analyze the genre, a vibrant entertainment scene and a large body of work were in existence.

The Most Influential Book in Storytelling

The scientist and philosopher Aristotle (384–322 BCE) was on a mission to understand everything and he made a good run at it. Aged 17 or 18 he came to Plato's academy in Athens and he was there for 20 years, until Plato died in 347.

He then went to Asia Minor and later to Lesbos where he got married and studied natural sciences. His work on zoology and marine biology was not surpassed in the following two millennia.

After 12 years he came back to Athens where he started his research institute, the Lyceum. He taught and wrote on metaphysics, ethics, rhetorics, history, and every other subject you can think of. Among these subjects was narrative poetry. He was fond of the tragedies of Sophocles and Euripides, who both died about 20 years before he was born, and the epic poems of Homer, who was about 400 years his senior.

During his lifetime he published—if this term makes sense in an era before printing—six books on Homeric problems and three on poets. These exoteric books, as they are called, were written as dialogues. The writing style was praised for its easy flow. Yet Aristotle's dialogues were viewed as a bit preachy and artistically inferior to those of his teacher Plato, who is rumored to have tried his hand at playwriting in his youth. The criticism that often befalls modern writing teachers also applies to Aristotle. He did not win tragedy competitions at the City Dionysia, and he was not an accomplished playwright in his own right.

The exoteric books are lost; none of them survived antiquity. Aristotle also wrote two unpublished, or esoteric, books on the subject: one on tragedy and one on comedy. They were likely meant for use internally in the Lyceum, either as lecture notes or as a textbook for students.

The book on comedy is lost. What we still have by him on the subject is the esoteric book on the tragedy, today known as his *Poetics*.

There is a discussion about whether the *Poetics* is an early or late work of Aristotle. Personally, I think the vision presented in the book seems mature, with the logical depth and coherence that is attained with time. There are parts on theatre history, the creative process, and literary criticism as well as on the construction of tragedies and epic poetry.

The book builds on and alludes to his work in other disciplines, like the exploration of the emotions in book two of his Rhetorics and actions in the Nicomachean ethics. But to see the Poetics as merely an abstract expression of his philosophy is a red herring. Aristotle's description of the tragedy is closer to real storytelling than it is to the reconstructions of his ideas attempted by scholars who subscribed to this view. The philosopher and scientist was out to crack the problem of the tragedy and he used the intellectual and scientific tools that were at his disposal.

The *Poetics* seems as though it has not been read much in antiquity. Although it figures in lists of his works, no commentary of it is known until those of the Arabic philosophers Avicenna (c. 980-1037) and Averroes (1126-1198).

The resurgence started in Italy during the

15th century when copies arrived there with Greek scholars who left the crumbling Byzantine empire. Before this the western world knew the *Poetics* through a latin translation of Averroes' commentary. Italy was a country with a rich literary tradition in both its own language and classical latin. Horace's *Ars Poetics* was already influential and misinterpreted. The commentary on *Poetics* picked up in the same vein.

This was not only due to misreading. The many generations of manual copying that had been necessary to preserve the book through the centuries introduced numerous errors. Additionally the copies that won wide circulation were not the most accurate. Scholars and scribes tried to fix problems by comparing versions, though not usually the most reliable ones, and by using their own good sense, a method referred to by modern scholars as *divination*. This resolved some inaccuracies, but introduced even more new ones.

During the 19th century, when one of the primary witnesses of the text was correctly identified, the reconstruction of the original text made progress. A primary witness is a copy that is not copied from an earlier original still in existence. Today we know four primary witnesses, the last one identified in the 1930s. Two are in Ancient Greek (10th and 12th century), one in Latin (12th century), and one is in Arabic (11th century). The Arabic was translated from an older Syric translation. The earliest split happened between the

Graeco-Latin branch and the Syro-Arabic, possibly sometime between the 4th and 6th century (Tarán, 2013, p. 35). Significant errors that can be traced back to the shared *archetype* are typical for the style of writing used during this period.

Today we have two editions of the Poetics in Ancient Greek that are reconstructed from all four primary witnesses. The first was made by Rudolph Kassel and was published in 1965. A recent one by Leonardo Tarán and Dimitri Gutas was published in 2012. These two critical editions signifies that today we have a more accurate approximation of the original text than has existed since antiquity.

Aristotle's *Poetics* is the beginning of literary theory and it continues to be the most cited text in the field. It is unique for a work this old to still play an active role in the academic debate.

The book has exerted a similar influence on practical storytelling, and is still read as a craft manual. In it you find the seeds of many, perhaps most, maxims practiced in modern storytelling. Both Hollywood directors who adhere to its principles and Brecht who rebelled against them found their own kind of inspiration in the book.

The influence goes at least back to Dante (c. 1265-1321) and the title of the *Divine Comedy*, which is a reference to the *Poetics* and the statement that comedies are about people that are worse than us. Schiller and Goethe both showed an active interest in Aristotle's text and wrote about it.

An interesting case is William Archer's book

Play-Writing from 1912 which ponders that Aristotle's beginning, middle, and end "would indicate the three-act division as the ideal scheme for a play". Archer refuses to be pedantic about ideal structures, but this passage may be the origin of "Aristotle's three act structure", which keeps popping up in screenwriting manuals (Lanouette, 1999). Archer makes many more references to Aristotle, and his book is an illustration of how modern craft manuals have absorbed ideas from the *Poetics*.

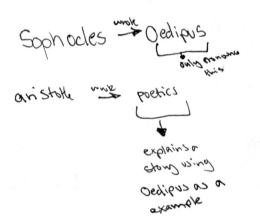

Sophocles → Oedipus
only mentions this

aristotle → poetics
explains a story using Oedipus as a example

The Untying

The Model in King Oedipus

The terse and abstract style of the *Poetics* makes it challenging to reconstruct Aristotle's ideas. To make it more concrete, it is useful to see how the techniques are used in the tragedies Aristotle analyzed.

Sophocles only came second in the City Dionysia of 427 BCE, the year he entered with *King Oedipus*. Yet the play is regarded as the masterpiece of ancient Greek tragedy. It is referenced no less than 10 times in the *Poetics*. Sometimes it is named the first whodunnit, which may seem a bit odd. The spectators know who did it almost from the start; the last one to figure it out is Oedipus himself. Still, the plot is constructed like that of a detective story.

King Oedipus uses many of the techniques Aristotle discusses, which is why it is the most referenced play in the book.

When *King Oedipus* begins, the terrible acts are already committed, the knot fully *tied*, and it has shown up in front of the royal palace in the form of a group of supplicants. Oedipus is still unaware of what he is about to *untie* as he steps out of the palace to meet them himself.

The elder of the group, a priest of Zeus, spares no gory detail as he elaborates how plague and blight are killing Thebes. He begs Oedipus—the first among men, solver of the riddle of the Sphinx,

and savior and king of Thebes—to free the city ~city~
from the *suffering*, setting the stakes as *serious*
indeed. Oedipus is already on the case. He has
sent Creon, his brother-in-law, as a messenger to
Delphi to consult the god Apollon, and he will do
whatever is required to free the city of the plague.
An *arc* away from plague and misery and towards
happiness for Thebes is set up.

As if on cue, Creon shows up the moment he is
mentioned. Apollon demands that the killing of
Laius is punished by death or exile.

Laius was the previous king of Thebes and the
first husband of Jocasta, Oedipus' wife. Oedipus
probes further, suspecting that the bandits were
paid by someone. He orders that the citizens of
Thebes show up in front of his palace, and when
they do, he tempts and threatens the guilty man
or anyone who knows his identity to stand forth.
When nobody does, somebody suggests that he
should call for the seer Tiresias.

Oedipus already has, and as he wonders why
the seer is not yet there, he arrives. Tiresias is unwilling to reveal anything about the wanted killer
of Laius. As Oedipus' rage about this treachery
against a city cursed by plague rises to the point
where he accuses Tiresias of being behind it himself, the seer gives in. He declares Oedipus the
killer. This *reversal* is offset a moment later, as
Oedipus *recognizes* the conspiracy. Creon is the
real culprit; he has teamed up with Tiresias to
usurp the throne. This *false recognition* leads to a

reversal where the *arc* turns towards *undeserved misfortune* for the *decent man* Creon, caused by a *mistake*.

The spectators cannot help but *pity* the poor fellow and *fear* for his fate.

Creon arrives to clear his name, but Oedipus sees only trickery in his words and is immovable. Oedipus is fully on the way to sentence him to death when Jocasta arrives to separate the two. She sends her brother away and speaks with her husband. He should not listen to seers, she comforts, and she starts telling an anecdote to illustrate how unreliable they are. An oracle predicted that Laius would be killed by his son, but he was not. He was killed by strangers at a place where three roads meet.

Oedipus falls absent, not hearing Jocasta tell of how the feet of their newborn son was pierced together and how he was put out to die by a servant.

The mention of the killing where three roads meet has reminded Oedipus of something. He probes further. Everything fits an incident that ended with Oedipus killing a man that struck him first. He wails in agony over the *recognition* that he might have killed Laius after all, making the moral stakes *serious*. There is just one detail. Oedipus was alone and Laius was killed by a group. Oedipus demands to speak with the servant who witnessed the incident, and Jocasta agrees to send for him. The *arc* has been *reversed* again, setting it towards securing Oedipus' *happiness* through clearing his name.

While waiting, Jocasta is worried about the mental state of her husband. She prays for the situation to be cleared up, creating a cue for the conspicuously timely arrival of a messenger from Corinth. Even here, with this unlikely coincidence, Sophocles tries to observe the *principle of probable or necessary consequence* and creates a preceding stimulus in the plot.

Polybos, King of Corinth and father of Oedipus, is dead and Oedipus is wanted to follow him on the throne.

Oedipus refuses to go to Corinth, however, as his mother Merope is still alive. An oracle has prophesied that he will kill his father and sleep with his mother. The natural death of his father frees him of the first concern, but there is still a chance of fulfilling the second.

The messenger eases him. He is not their child by birth. A shepherd gave a baby with his feet pierced together to the messenger, and he brought the baby to the childless Polybos and Merope, who adopted Oedipus.

Oedipus wonders who the shepherd with the baby is. He was a servant of Laius, the messenger says. The baby had his feet pierced together. Oedipus asks Jocasta if she knows him, but she refuses to say, and spectators who listened to her when Oedipus did not earlier see that she has *recognized* who he is and what is about to happen (Poetics, 10/52a24). When he presses, she flees. Oedipus makes the *mistake* of thinking that she is afraid that she has married a beggar, and decides to press on. The *arc* is *reversed* towards undeserved moral agony as the spectators, like Jocasta, see that Oedipus is headed for an unpleasant discovery.

The eyewitness to the murder of Laius shows up. The messenger *recognizes* him as the man who gave him the baby. Oedipus presses the shepherd on who he got the baby from. He does not want to say but gives in under threats of violence. He got the baby from Jocasta to set it out to die, because it was prophesied that the baby would kill his father. Oedipus has fled from the prophecies in vain; they have been fulfilled to the word. The moral agony of the final *recognition* hits Oedipus with force.

He storms out and finds Jocasta already dead. She has hung herself in the bedchamber. He pierces his own eyes out with her brooch. The finality of the acts resolves the threats, although unhappily. The tension is *purged* and perhaps replaced in the spectators with emotional numbness and a sense of inner calm. Oedipus falls from king to beggar, all authority lost. His brother-in-law denies him even the right to chose his misfortune and refuses to grant his wish of exile.

Aristotle's Model

Let us look at the main concepts of Aristotle's model of the tragedy and how they fit together.

The tragedy has *plot* and persons with *character*. The persons reveal their *character* (ethos) through choices and by showing preferences. If all actions and speech spring logically from the situations alone the tragedy does not have character. If the actions makes us characterize the persons as for example clever or suspicious types, it does. The persons should act in ways that are *necessary or probable* according to their character.

The *plot* (muthos) *emulates* an *action*. Like a real *action*, the *plot* has a motivation, which is derived from a circumstantial knot and a purpose towards solving the knot. The choice of method and the intention behind this choice gives the *action* a moral quality.

It is more important that the *plot* is well developed than that the *characters* are. This follows from the aims of tragedy, which are to *emulate* an *action* and to evoke *pity and fear*.

The *action* (praxis) emulated by the *plot* should:

- Be *serious-and-good*. It should be well-intentioned or at least justifiable in the situation, and something important should be at stake.
- Be *complete*. It should have a beginning, middle and end. The exact understanding of where an action begins and ends is part of the philosophical challenge posed to poets.
- Have a *certain magnitude*. The knot should neither be too complex nor be too easily untied, and something important should be at stake.
- Evoke *pity and fear*. This is the feeling some-

one has when witnessing an accident about to happen to someone they care for and they are powerless to avert it.

- *Purge* the tension by resolving the threats for a good or bad outcome, thereby completing the action.

What-is-suffered, the *situation* or the *trauma* (pathos), typically threats of violence, plague, etc., make the stakes serious. The threatened loss of *family and friends* (philia) does the same.

A *decent* (epieikes) person is one who does not intentionally inflict undeserved misfortune and therefore does not deserve misfortune.

A *wicked* (phaulos) person is one who intentionally inflicts undeserved misfortune and therefore deserves misfortune.

Pity (eleos) is evoked by the present or threatened *undeserved misfortune*, perhaps the loss of *family and friends*.

Sympathy or *support* (philantropos) is evoked by the present or expected end of *undeserved misfortune*, perhaps through the resolution of an evil threat.

The *plot* should have a causality chain that runs from the beginning to the end. This implies that the actions should be logical in the situation as well as for the *character* of the person. The *plot* of a tragedy has one causal chain, or *middle*, connecting the beginning and end. The epic poem, which is longer and can have parallel plot lines, has several *middles*.

The *tying* (desis) ties the knot. The tying starts at the beginning of the back story and lasts until the point in the plot where a motivation for solving the knot is set up, early in the play.

The *untying* (lusis) of the knot starts from where the tying ends and runs to the end.

The *arc* (metabasis) runs alongside the *untying* and moves either towards or away from misfortune. The plot only has one *arc*, even if the conflict is two-sided. It is defined by how the emulated action affects the side the spectators root for.

A *plot* without twists in the *arc* through *reversals* or changes in the understanding of the knot through *recognitions* is simple. A *plot* with them is complex. Complex is better.

A *reversal* (peripeteia) will change the direction of the *arc*, making it go towards misfortune if it was moving away, and vice versa. *Reversals* should be surprising but logical. They raise tension.

A *recognition* (anagnorisis) will change the understanding of the knot in an important way, for example, through the discovery that a believed stranger or enemy is really family. *Recognitions* should be surprising but logical, and like *reversals* they raise tension. A *recognition* has more impact when combined with a *reversal*.

We feel *sympathy towards* or *root for* (philantropos) actions that fight undeserved misfortune.

Actions that intend undeserved misfortune are *repulsive* (miaron).

A well-intentioned or justified action that is

headed towards misfortune because of a *mistake* (hamartia) is the most tragic, as this is the only one that evokes pity. The lack of wicked intention makes the expected outcome undeserved. The mistake must be visible to the spectators but not the person making the mistake.

Suffered threats can be resolved (from worst to best) by fizzling out, or by being acted out, or—if a *mistake* is involved—by being committed and then *recognized*, or by being averted through a last moment *recognition*.

The *purging* (katharsis) of *pity and fear* is achieved when the final threat is resolved, completing the action and making the play end.

The Four Sources of Dramatic Pleasure

Aristotle divides the tragedy into four main components that we can call sources of dramatic pleasure. These are *mimetic form*, *character*, *pathos*, and *action*, which translates into artistic portrayals of people in trouble trying to find a way out. Or, if we use more Aristotelian terms, stage shows or narrative poems about persons who are tied into a knot and trying to untie it. In the context of the tragedy the hard to translate *pathos* is traumatic, but a more neutral translation would be an emotionally charged situation or experience. A genre neutral, and very useful, listing of the four sources of dramatic pleasure could then be *mimetic form*, *character*, *situation* and *action*.

The division is mentioned only in passing. First

for dance in *Poetics* 1, then for tragedy in a somewhat cryptic reference in *Poetics* 18. Each of the four sources has a corresponding type of tragedy that specializes in it, but the ideal tragedy excels in all four. It has breathtaking stage show, dilemmas that reveal character, action with logical but surprising twists, and a knot that sets deadly stakes. In *Poetics* 24 the sources are discussed for epic poetry. The *Iliad* and the *Odyssey* between them demonstrate excellence in the use of two kinds of action, character, pathos and two elements of form—reason (rhetorical speech) and language.

The passing mention indicates that Aristotle considers the four sources to be prior knowledge for students of his advanced course on *Poetics*, and it seems likely that the division was part of the craft terminology at the time.

Aristotle dedicates more space to the division of the tragedy into six parts that can be studied in isolation: plot construction, character, reasoning, language, music, and stage show. They correspond to fields of scientific inquiry, but do not map directly to the four sources. Some fields study many sources and some sources are studied by many fields.

- Plot construction is the art of organizing incidents with pathos, action, and sometimes character in order to achieve emotional impact. This is a main subject of the *Poetics*.
- Character is how actions—and through them the persons performing them—differ and can be assigned qualities according to certain cri-

teria. It is related to ethics.

- Reasoning is typically rhetorical speech giving a person's analysis of the situation or an attempt at convincing someone about facts. This could be considered as part of the action, but Aristotle groups it with language in *Poetics* 24, indicating that he sees it as part of the mimetic form. It falls under rhetorics.
- Language, music, and stage show are parts of the mimetic form.

The scientific dissection leads to a definition in *Poetics* 6 which states that the tragedy is the emulation of an action that should evoke pity and fear. This goal must be reached through the four sources of dramatic pleasure. To achieve this the poet must at least make a good knot and untie it well, with added points for creating interesting characters.

It is also possible to achieve it through the stage show. With music, dance, masks, and stage machinery, one can imagine a feast for the senses. Seeing *Prometheus* on stage chained to a stone with a spike through his chest must have been a pitiful image. But this falls outside the poetic art.

Tragic Mimesis

Aristotle places the tragedy among the mimetic arts, which includes painting, sculpture and dance, as well as poetry and drama. The word *mimesis* is a hard one to translate. It has a wider meaning than our equivalents (Halliwell, 1986, chapter IV); modern English terms have not evolved to capture the characteristics of *mimesis* that are important to Aristotle. This makes it impossible to find one translation that works in all contexts, even inside the *Poetics*.

Both the creation of *mimesis* and the fascination for watching one is in our nature (Poetics 4).

We take our first steps of learning through *mimesis*. Here it is interesting to note that learning to walk or speak is not just a matter of superficial imitation. Walking requires coordination and balance acquired through practical trial and error. The learning has happened when a higher mastery or deeper understanding has been reached. Seeing how important *mimesis* is to our development, there is little wonder that we are attracted to the creative process offered by mimetic arts. Essentially, it is the same thing.

Our fascination for watching a *mimesis* is proven by the fact that we like to look at paintings even of things that would repel us in real life—like disgusting insects or dead bodies. Even non-philosophers like to figure things out, and recognizing what is in a painting appeals to this instinct. Here it is interesting to note that the ability to translate sensory information into concepts is vital for us. Even the most mundane activities depend on them. Again, there is little wonder that it excites pleasure and that we are intrigued as spectators.

In the context of a narrative art, like tragedy, *figuring out* means understanding the situation. The events that are played out in front of the spectators are organized in their mind. If a piece of backstory is revealed, it is placed where it belongs in the chronology. Narratologists like to point out that you can tell a story backward, and the listeners will reorganize it in their mind and make it chronological. But this is not the only kind of mapping that takes place. Pieces of information are tagged as credible or not. At a given point contradicting versions of a past event can be presented as true. Threats, opportunities, and possible futures are identified. As are allies, enemies, and social hierarchies. Characters are attributed with traits and moral qualities. While the *mimesis* is played out, the understanding of the situation changes. Things are added, changed, or even removed. Threats, alliances, and truth are all in flux.

The spectators build and modify a mental model of the world of the *mimesis* in the same way as they do of reality based on real experiences.

A poet differs from a natural scientist in that he composes a *mimesis*. A natural scientist presents us with an already constructed model, explaining it rather than making the audience derive it themselves. A poet creates a *mimesis* (*Poetics* 1) that is played out and which leaves it up to the spectators to construct a model what is going on.

Poets like Homer and Sophocles takes this a step further. They step into their characters' minds and envision the model of reality that has evolved in them from their experiences. Aristotle may be alluding to this when he says that poets should speak as little as possible in their own voice (*Poetics* 24). When words and actions spring out of the characters' mental processes, rather than an observing narrator's, it gives depth to the *mimesis*, and the better the poet is able to do this, the deeper it is.

Aristotle touches upon this aspect of *mimesis* when he discusses the difference between history and tragedy (*Poetics* 8). History is about what happened. Tragedy is about what could happen—the universal principles of necessary and probable consequence that govern what a person with a certain character will do in a situation.

This makes the tragedy akin to philosophy, Aristotle says. It makes it akin to psychology, sociology, and other disciplines interested in why and how we act the way we do as well. But it is worth noting that while the first loyalty of science is the accurate recording of facts, the first concern of the tragic poet is the unity of the whole. The scientist searches for the universal by investigating and testing against the specific. The poet gives depth and nuance to the whole by finding and adding specifics that belong. The parts are true when the whole rings true.

The philosophical dimension applies to the whole as well as the parts. King Oedipus has a plot with an almost perfect causal chain. This creates an illusion of control for the characters. But the spectators see something else. However much Oedipus tries to flee the prophecy the finger of fate is there, leading him back on its path through "coincidences". Sophocles' point is that we always

28

and inevitably act on insufficient information, and he takes this to the hypothetical extreme by having Oedipus do exactly the things he tries to avoid.

The *mimetic* process is a loop. We switch between a mimetic mode where we create and a receptive mode where we review. In the receptive mode, we may sense that something is wrong. But fixing it requires understanding. We must find and grasp the universal principle we have violated. Perhaps the character's behavior rings false because of a problem in the psychology?

Usually, translations of the *Poetics* translate *mimesis* to imitation or representation. Of the two I prefer imitation. You could imitate a skylark by singing like one, while the bird is represented by the word *skylark*. Imitation is a likeness, representation a symbol. The tragedy is more likeness than symbol.

One discussion that arises from this translation is that imitation implies a real original. This question is not important to Aristotle. The tragedy can be historical or fictitious. What matters is that the poet is able to construct a plot that complies with the universal principles of necessary or probable consequence—an aspect that is captured by neither of the two terms.

More promising in this regard are the words simulation and emulation. Both words imply movement, so they will not work for sculpture or painting, but they are a good fit for the tragedy. A simulation begins with a theoretical model and plays out a scenario, much like Aristotle wants the tragedy to do.

But simulation underplays the imitative aspect. It would be more correct to say that a child learns by emulating a model rather than by simulating one. The tragedian will not start with a theory, but with a story idea, and they will fix it until it works, like a child learning to walk. We could say that the tragedy aspires to imitate the key dynamics of something, which is what is suggested by emulation.

The Plot Emulates an Action

Aristotle defines the tragedy as the emulation of an action. This action he names plot. He puts forth a number of requirements for it. It should be whole, have a certain magnitude, be good and serious, evoke pity and fear, and resolve the tension at the end.

But he never says exactly what an action is.

This omission is deliberate and interesting. Tragedians are not there to always demonstrate the same definition of action. Their task is to explore what an action is in the specific context of their story.

Giving an exact definition of action would be telling the tragedian what to say. That would be the same as telling a philosopher what to think. This perspective is interesting in today's scene of formulaic writing manuals. Aristotle pinpointed the characteristics that he thought important for a tragedy to work. But he left it at that. He did not create a blueprint for storytellers to copy.

What he offered was a study of how to evoke an emotional reaction in the spectators. At its heart his *Poetics* is about spectator psychology.

Still, a concrete and sophisticated model of the action is implied, perhaps because it is implied by the tragedies Aristotle studied. That the tragedy should emulate a single action does not, as one could easily think, dictate that the plot should follow a single person. What is meant is that the plot has the same characteristics as an action.

So what are these?

One requirement is that the action should be whole, and a whole action has a beginning. But where exactly does an action begin?

You may have your own answer to this. But for now let us consult someone who put a lot of thought into the question, John Dewey, who is often considered the greatest American philosopher. In *Experience and Education* (chapter 6), he says that the formulation of a goal (or purpose) starts with an impulse that when obstructed turns into a desire. This desire motivates an investigation of the situation that ends in the formulation of a goal, a plan.

If we read this in the context of another thinker, the psychologist Abraham Maslow, we could say that the impulse comes from a need. The need for safety, perhaps, or some kind of social need. When the impulse is blocked, the need is blocked, which explains why it becomes a desire.

The tragedies usually start with setting up a situation where an impulse or need is blocked and turned into a desire.

John Dewey's observation could have been taken from a writing manual. But his concern was not how to begin a plot. He was concerned with how to engage students by having them work on tasks.

The wonder of it is that a spectator will become engaged much in the same way if the problem is properly introduced to them and they empathize with the person who must solve it. This is why Aristotle says the plot emulates an action. Watching a tragedy evokes emotions in us through the same mechanisms as witnessing or participating in a real action would.

The implications of this insight are great. It moves plotting out of the realm of copying blueprints and into the realm of psychology. If you understand what actions are, why we get engaged in them and how they are interesting to us, you can start thinking for yourself.

On the other hand, there is also reason to respect the blueprints. They have found their form because they work, which means there is cognitive knowledge hidden in them. This makes them worth studying, not necessarily to use them, but to find these hidden lessons—which is more or less what Aristotle did with the tragedy.

The Circumstantial Knot

The villain is not part of Aristotle's model of the tragedy. There is a reason for this. Aristotle does not think that conflicts which depict good versus bad are the best fit for the tragic genre. Instead, he favors a more universal concept. The circumstantial knot.

Since the plot is the emulation of an action, it follows that it should have a purpose. We act because of something and to achieve something. In a tragedy this something is the circumstantial knot.

The knot is implied by the discussion of the tying (*desis*) and the untying (*lusis*) in *Poetics* 18 (55b24). A little later in the chapter he comments that many poets make a good knot (*ploke*), but untie it badly. He sometimes uses *knot* as a metaphor for an unsolved problem in other works as well, like the Metaphysics (995a10).

There are two kinds of knots (Poetics 13/53a12). The double structure or double interest knot pits sides with opposite interests against each other. This knot sets enemy against enemy. Aristotle mentions Homer's epic poem *Odyssey* as an example of a double interest knot. Odysseus must stop the suitors before they eat him to poverty and kill his son.

The single structure or single interest knot has no real conflict of interest, but a mistake makes it seem so to the parties involved. This knot pits friend against friend (*Poetics* 14/54b15). The spectators must be initiated in the mistake. If not, it is effectively a double interest knot until they are. If the threatened *pathos* is undeserved the spectators feel pity for the involved and want the *pathos* averted.

The knot of many tragedies have what we may call *motivational pathos*. Pathos is a difficult concept in the *Poetics* for an ironic reason. Aristotle hardly bothers to explain it, probably because he considers it an elementary concept that is already known. It is often translated as *suffering*, but based on Aristotle's definition, *trauma* seems to be a better fit. It is defined as *death, bodily agony, wounds and the like* which is *open to sight* (*Poetics* 11). Storytellers in less violent genres might choose to see *pathos* as a metaphor for something less drastic.

Pathos plays an important role in evoking the tragic emotions pity and fear, which is an aim of tragedy.

Pity is evoked by undeserved misfortune (Poetics 13). Undeserved is a moral judgement. A person is percieved as too good to deserve this. Misfortune implies *pathos* or emotional pain. Pity is related to empathy.

Fear is evoked by imagining an impending evil of a destructive or painful kind (Rhetorics 2.5) against ourselves or someone we identify with. This implies a threat of future *pathos*, and as the threat somehow must enter the imagination of the spectators, it must be *open to sight*. Fear is related to suspense.

In *King Oedipus* the plague that ravages Thebes serves as a *motivational pathos*. When the untying of it is obstructed, there is a pressure cooker effect, that builds up to what one might call *climactic pathos*. When Tiresias refuses to supply information that will solve the murder that is causing the plague, the episode becomes confrontational. Oedipus starts to threaten Tiresias. This *climactic pathos* is averted by a reversal when Tiresias gives in and reveals that Oedipus himself is the murderer he is looking for.

In *King Oedipus* there is *pathos* in almost every episode and it is used in all manner of sophisticated ways. The motivational and climactic pathos changes from episode to episode. It is used for evoking pity, fear, or both at the same time. It has happened in the past, is ongoing, or threatened in the future.

The plague that ravages Thebes is an ongoing *motivational pathos*. It sets the stakes high and creates urgency for finding a solution by evoking pity for the citizens. It also makes us root for Oedipus, because his intention to help them out of their misfortune is good.

The past *pathos* of the murder of king Laius has never been solved. It is the cause of the plague, which makes it important to find the murderer. Oedipus makes the point that he himself could be the next victim, turning the past *pathos* into a threat of future *pathos*. This makes it a potential source of fear, at least for himself.

The past *pathos* of Oedipus' feet being pierced together when he was a baby does not evoke fear, as it carries no future threat with it. But it evokes empathy and perhaps even pity for Oedipus.

There are several threats of future *climactic pathos*. Creon is threatened with a death penalty. The threat is undeserved, so it evokes pity. Sophocles uses it to create confrontation and build tension towards an episode climax. Although the *pathos* is averted by Jocasta, the threat does its job during the episode. The episode with Tiresias is constructed in the same way.

The knot must have the right complexity. A suitable number of steps should be required to untie it. A longer narrative, like an epic poem, can have a larger and more complex knot, but Aristotle warns against making it too large. Homer did not make an epic about the whole Trojan war, he picked a specific part to focus on.

As the plot should emulate a single action with a single end (*Poetics* 24), it follows that there should be a single knot. This does not mean that the whole knot must be known from the start. The tying of the knot happens for the most part outside the plot, in the back story. This invites the poet to tie an iceberg knot, where much of the knot is out of sight for the spectators at the beginning, and then slowly revealed as events unfold.

Sometimes the tying continues a bit into the plot, until a motivation for the action has been set up.

In *Iphigenia among the Taurians* Euripides has Iphigenia step out in front of the spectators to explain the knot to them directly. When she has introduced it to them, the real action starts.

In *King Oedipus* Sophocles sets up a tiny initial knot—a group of supplicants has shown up in front of his palace—and lets the situation escalate. In this way he is able to start the untying instantly. The knot that has been tied in the backstory is large, but the full complexity of it is revealed by the untying action throughout the play, one recognition at the time.

In the definition of the tragedy Aristotle states that the action should be serious and have a certain magnitude. The magnitude is a product of the weight and size, or *pathos* and complexity, of the knot. The seriousness is a product of the magnitude.

Intention, Arc, and Climax

When the initial knot—or to be more precise, an arc towards a better or worse situation has been set up—the untying starts. The successful untying, or positive resolution of the motivational *pathos*, is what the spectators root for.

The untying action is either succeeding or failing. The trajectory towards better or worse we can call the arc. It is an imprecise term, but it is hard to find one that covers the underlying concept accurately. The Greek term is change (*metabasis*), which is imprecise as well. It is not a completed change, it is an expected change. It is the change the spectators hope for or fear. The prospective change.

The arc should not be flat. It should either point towards a better or worse situation—preferably much better or much worse. For tragedies, which Aristotle says should evoke pity and fear through a negative arc, he recommends that the person should be famous and fortunate.

In addition, the untying action has a moral quality, which decides whether the spectators will empathize with it or not. Without any laws or rules to guide us we have an ability to intuit right from wrong (*Rhetoric* 1.13) and our sense of what is undeserved and therefore pitiable is hardwired to this moral instinct.

Poetics 13 and 14 discusses actions with different intentions and arcs and how spectators respond to them.

Intending to harm someone decent is repulsive. In a plot with a double interest knot this is often exploited to make the spectators root against someone and set them out as bad. Hospitality was one of the pillars of Greek society in Homeric times, and abusing it, as the suitors do in the Odyssey, was a crime that rooted the listeners against them. Sometimes the person that spectators root for can intend such an action. An example is when Medea plans to kill her children to get back at her unfaithful husband in Euripides' tragedy of the same name. The spectators find the action itself repulsive, but the threatened fulfillment can evoke pity and fear. When an action with this intention is dominant the situation is headed towards worse and the arc of the plot is negative.

Usually the side the spectators root for has the opposite intention. It tries to bring down the bad side. As the bad are those harming the good, this amounts to the same as helping the good side, which may be why this is not listed as a separate plot type. This appeals to our moral sense, and the spectators will root for a positive outcome (*philantropia*). The prospective fulfillment of this action will not evoke pity and fear, although a real or imagined counter action by the bad side may. A plot with this purpose has a positive arc and Aristotle sees it as more in the spirit of comedy than tragedy.

These two kinds of actions are the main building blocks of a plot based on a double interest knot that pits a good side against a bad. Stories where a clever villain, like Sisyphus, is outwitted (*Poetics* 18), may serve as an example. Such plots build up to a climax that leads to opposite outcomes for the good and the bad. In comedies mortal enemies sometimes make up their differences with a happy ending for all.

An action with the intention of helping the bad side neither evokes enthusiasm nor leads to a climactic moment that evokes pity and fear, and Aristotle considers it as the most useless in the construction of plots.

Aristotle does not consider any of these actions to be tragic. He wants an action that evokes pity in itself, rather than only through the intended outcome. This can be achieved through an action with good intentions, but due to a mistake (*hamartia*), is headed towards a horrible outcome. An audience who is aware of the mistake will both sympathize with the intention and be filled with pity and fear over the approaching outcome. It should set friend against friend, as killing an enemy by mistake does not evoke pity. This action has a single interest knot, there are no winners, only losers.

An example from *King Oedipus* is when Oedipus wrongly infers that Tiresias and Creon is conspiring against him and he wants to sentence Creon to death. The action is justifiable as the intention is self defense, but the outcome would be that Oedipus kills his most loyal ally and that Creon undeservedly loses his life.

The mistake plot is Aristotle's preferred plot for the tragedy, and he advises poets to build the plays on myths with traumatic incidents between family members.

These can either be told in the fashion of the old poets, who built up to a climax where the violence was committed in full knowledge. The act is repulsive, but the threatened outcome is pitiful. An example is found in Euripides' *Medea* when Medea kills her children.

Or it can be committed in ignorance, as in the backstory of *King Oedipus*, where Oedipus kills his father. Causing harm with or without intent makes a lot of difference. Where the first act is repulsive, the second is pitiable. The whole of Oedipus builds up to the startling recognition that follows.

The best climax is when the mistake is averted through a last moment recognition, like in the conspiracy episodes with Tiresias and Creon in *King Oedipus*. Or even more elegantly, like in *Iphigenia among the Taurians*, where the horrible act is averted when Iphigenia recognizes that the person she is about to have sacrificed is her own brother.

Twisted Plots

Some actions are simple. You look at the problem, formulate a plan, execute it, and the problem is fixed. Or not. In both cases the outcome is final.

But some are not so straightforward. When you execute the plan, you find that it does not work. Perhaps you misunderstood the problem, or you did not have enough information, or you misjudged your ability, or any number of things. You have to look at the problem again, formulate a new plan, and try anew. And if this fails too, repeat until you find a solution or accept defeat.

In the same way, there are simple and complex plots (Poetics 10). In simple plots, the knot and the arc are set up in the beginning, and then they stay stable to the end, where the situation is resolved. Perhaps with a final catastrophe, breakthrough or twist.

The complex plot, however, is full of twists caused by recognitions and reversals that should both be surprising and a logical consequence of what has preceded (*Poetics* 11).

We may view this in light of Aristotle's discussion of master activities and subordinate activities in the *Nicomachean Ethics* (1094a8). The goal of a master action, which in the case of a plot is the untying of the knot, is sometimes pursued through subordinate actions and goals. If the sequence of subordinate actions are spawned or completed as a result of recognitions or reversals, Aristotle calls the plot complex.

The *Nicomachean* perspective invites us see the plot as nesting lesser actions inside higher, enabling us to assess the aim and moral quality of each action and each layer separately, and additionally to think of lesser actions that build up to reversals or recognitions as simple plots inside the complex. Aristotle does not address this explicitly in the *Poetics*, but his allusion to complex actions should probably be interpreted in this direction.

Recognitions *(anagnorisis)* are a change from ignorance to knowledge. Aristotle's main example being that the true identity of someone becomes clear, moving them towards friendship or enmity. Recognitions have a stronger impact if they trigger a reversal.

Reversals *(peripeteia)* flip the arc. If it was headed towards a better situation, it starts heading towards a worse, and vice versa. Frequent reversals take spectators on an emotional roller coaster trip. In one moment they feel hopeful suspense and in the next pitiful fear for the characters they root for.

In *King Oedipus* each of the four episodes contains a major recognition. The first three of them are evenly spaced, at around line 378, 731 and 1056 of 1530, while the fourth and final recognition comes quickly after the third, at about 1180.

The first major recognition happens about one-fourth into the play. Oedipus consults the seer Tiresias about who killed King Laius. Tiresias is reluctant to say anything. This angers Oedipus to the extent that he accuses Tiresias of being behind the act. Tiresias responds by claiming that Oedipus himself is the killer and, additionally, that he lives in shame. This leads Oedipus to the conclusion that Creon has conspired with Tiresias to overthrow him and take his throne (Berg-Clay, lines 464-547).

The recognition conforms both to Aristotle's principle that a recognition should be logical in hindsight (Poetics 9/52a4) and that it should change the emotional tie between two important characters towards friendship or enmity (Poetics 9/52a32). The man Oedipus thought was his closest ally and friend is discovered to be his worst enemy and a threat to the throne.

The conclusion is surprising, but it is consistent with the facts already revealed in the play. Creon has been in a position to engineer the situation. Oedipus is sure he never met Laius, and he has already shown a tendency to see conspiracies.

The new insight shifts the focus of Oedipus away from finding the killer of Laius and towards addressing the conspiracy against his own person.

This shift in the main motivation and goal is a major redefinition of the knot. Aristotle does not make this point, but Sophocles is hardly unaware of it.

As described, this is already fine use of recognition. But the moment has another layer. The recognition is false. The change from "ignorance" to "knowledge" is subjective.

The false recognition causes Oedipus to accuse Creon of treason and to sentence him to a death penalty. This is an example of the famous, but poorly understood, mistake plot that Aristotle speaks of in Poetics 13: "What remains, is the case between, where a man is pushed towards misfortune not in spite of virtue, or because of vice, but because of a mistake (*hamartia*)."

Pity is evoked by undeserved misfortune (Poetics 13/54a4). The fact that the decent Creon stands innocently accused makes the spectators feel pity for him, and they want to see his death penalty averted. The positive arc towards a cure for Thebes is replaced with a negative arc towards injustice for Creon, which means that the recognition has come together with a reversal, as Aristotle recommends.

The second major recognition happens near the midpoint of the play. Creon has tried to convince Oedipus that it would be stupid for him to usurp the throne. He already has all the advantages of the position through his relation to Oedipus and his sister, Queen Jocasta, while not having to look over his shoulder for conspiracies.

Oedipus remains unconvinced. In the end, Jocasta comes in and separates her quarreling husband and brother. She sends her brother away and tries to calm her husband down.

JOCASTA: What started your quarrel?

OEDIPUS: He said I murdered Laius.

JOCASTA: Does he know something? Or is it pure hearsay?

OEDIPUS: He sent me a vicious, trouble-making prophet / to avoid implicating himself. He did not say it to my face.

JOCASTA: Oedipus, forget all this. Listen to me: / no mortal can practice the art of prophecy, no man can see the future. / One experience of mine will show you why. / Long ago an oracle came to Laius. / It came not from Apollo himself but from his priests. / It said Laius was doomed to be murdered by a son, his son and mine. / But Laius, from what we heard, was murdered by bandits from a foreign country, / cut down at a crossroads. My poor baby / was only three days old when Laius had his feet pierced together behind the ankles / and gave orders to abandon our child on a mountain, leave him alone to die / in a wilderness of rocks and bare gray trees / where there were no roads, no people. / So you see —Apollo didn't make that child his father's killer, / Laius wasn't murdered by his son. That dreadful act which so terrified Laius— / it never happened. All those oracular voices meant was nothing, nothing. / Ignore them. / Apollo creates. Apollo reveals. He needs no help from men.

OEDIPUS (who has been very still): While you were speaking, Jocasta; it flashed through my mind / like wind suddenly ruffling a stretch of calm sea. / It stuns me. I can almost see it —some memory, some image. / My heart races and swells—

JOCASTA: Why are you so strangely excited, Oedipus?

OEDIPUS: You said Laius was cut down near a crossroads?

(Stein Berg-Diskin Clay translation, 928-956)

Her mention of where Laius was killed makes Oedipus remember something. He interrogates her, and everything she says matches his memory.

OEDIPUS: (...) Jocasta, the story I'm about to tell you is the truth: / I was on the road, near the crossroads you mentioned, / when I met a herald, with an old man, just as you described him. / The man was riding in a chariot / and his driver tried to push me off the road / and when he shoved me I hit him. / I hit him. The old man stood quiet in the chariot until I passed under him, / then he leaned out and caught me on the head with an ugly goad— / its two teeth wounded me —and with this hand of mine, / this hand clenched around my staff, / I struck him back even harder —so hard, so quick he couldn't dodge it, / and he toppled out of the chariot and hit the ground, face up. / I killed them. Every one of them. I still see them.

(Berg-Clay, 1039-1051)

The recognition opens Oedipus up to the possibility that Tiresias spoke the truth, that he actually killed Laius. Only one detail does not match. The one surviving eyewitness, now a shepherd, said Laius was killed by a group of bandits. Oedipus was alone.

The moment does not conform well with Aristotle's requirement that a recognition should move a relation to friendship or enmity. Oedipus is moved from certainty to uncertainty. His relation with Creon moves away from enmity, but not quite to friendship. His relation with himself moves away from love, but not yet to hate.

Anagnorisis and *peripeteia* may have been technical playwriting terms in the ancient Greek theatre. If so, one gets the impression that Sophocles' definition of recognition would be different from Aristotle's. Aristotle focuses on how it changes the ties between characters to affection or hate. Sophocles uses recognition to redefine the knot. When it comes to emotional consequences, he is more nimble and sensitive to story needs than Aristotle's requirement allows. But Aristotle himself makes the point that there are many types of recognitions, and explicitly mentions a use of recognition by token for confirming identity. The one changing a relation to friendship or enmity is just the one that best helps the plot to have an emotional impact.

After the midpoint recognition, Oedipus' focus turns away from the conspiracy and towards learning the truth about himself. A little short of three-quarters through the play, there is yet another recognition, which is mentioned in the *Poetics* (10/52a24) as an example of how to combine recognition and reversal. The pieces are falling in place. It is becoming clear that Oedipus is the son of Jocasta and Laius; he has killed his father and bred children with his mother.

Jocasta sees this, and it is her recognition that Aristotle speaks of. She begs Oedipus to stop his investigations. But he refuses. When she runs away, he falsely infers that she is just worried that she will discover that her husband is really a son of poor people. This leads to a reversal of the positive arc towards clearing his name to a negative mistake arc, as in the episode with Tiresias.

Oedipus repeats the recognition of his mother in the short fourth episode. The recognition is handled in the spirit of Aristotle; a loved one becomes an enemy, but again with a twist. The loved one is Oedipus himself.

Aristotle lists a number of ways that a recognition may come about (Poetics 16/54b19). Sophocles uses most of them in *King Oedipus*. Oedipus' feet are marked, a messenger arrives, Oedipus remembers, he infers that Creon conspires, and Jocasta and Oedipus see the pieces falling in place as a consequence of the plot.

When it comes to the effect of the recognition, Aristotle says there should be a change towards affection or hate between important characters. This looks more like a special case than a definition of recognition. Sophocles shows us that recognitions may build up to any dramatic effect.

Necessary and Likely Consequence

Aristotle states that the plot should emulate an action that is complete. It follows that it should have a beginning that is connected, through a middle, to an end, and the connection should be by necessary or likely consequence (Poetics 7/50b23).

For the tragedy Aristotle specifies a singular middle, meaning a plot with only one causal chain or plot line. Epic poems, which sometimes have parallel plot lines, are defined as having plural middles (Poetics 23/59a19). As long as they are relevant to the story as a whole, parallel plot lines have some advantages. They enable variation, for example. Aristotle believes them not possible in the tragedy because of logistical constraints of the stage (Poetics 24/59b29).

The practical consequence is that the actions of the characters should be logical in light of what has already happened in the plot. This is the first cause of actions.

In addition, Aristotle specifies that persons should be consistent and act in ways that are necessary or plausible for their character. This means that their character is a second cause.

There is one that is not mentioned explicitly. The plot follows the untying of a circumstantial knot. This knot is tied outside the plot, and parts of it may be hidden for the persons and the spectators for parts of the play. Though it is not mentioned explicitly, the knot is the third cause.

This is what we can infer or what is explicitly stated in the *Poetics*. Aristotle does not describe in detail how the causality actually works. There is a reason for this. He considers it the philosophical task of the poet and the individual tragedy to discover and explore these principles in the context of the plot.

But we can study how Sophocles did it in Aristotle's favorite play, *King Oedipus*. The play begins like this:

An actor sits on the stage, close to spectators, dressed like a priest, wearing the mask of Zeus. He holds branches wound in wool, a wreath is on his head and he sings a hymn to the gods. A group of young boys sits around him. The chorus sings with him from backstage.

Behind him stage paintings show a city in the background and trees. The stage house has the royal emblem of Thebes, showing that it is the palace.

Through the palace door comes a second actor, dressed like a king, and wearing the mask of a king. He stops and looks at the priest, then at the left stage entrance, as if looking for someone. His gaze returns to the priest and the boys, and he walks towards them.

The priest stops singing, raises his hands, as if in fear, and kneels. The boys follow his example.

The king stops. "Why, children," he says, addressing spectators behind the priest, "why are you here, why / are you holding those branches tied with wool, / begging me for help? Children, / the whole city smolders with incense. / Wherever I go I hear sobbing, praying. Groans fill the air. Rumors, news from messengers, they are not enough for me. / Others cannot tell me what you need. / I am king, I had to come. As king, I had to know. Know for myself, know for me. Everybody everywhere knows who I am: Oedipus. King."

There is already a lot going on here. Why is the group comprised of either children, young men or old priests? Are they afraid of offending the king if they show up with a brash crowd? Are they appealing to his compassion? They are not rushing into the palace, demanding the king's attention. They are just sitting there, in his yard, praying to the gods. How could he be offended? One can sense the planning that has gone into this.

This is clearly not the beginning of the causal chain for either Oedipus or those praying. So what is Aristotle speaking about with his beginning? Is his favorite play failing to conform to his requirements by starting at random and in middle of things?

No. Although this is not the beginning of the causal chain for Oedipus or for those praying, it is for the spectators. The person Oedipus is expecting is not allowed by the playwright to arrive yet because we do not know why he should arrive. The motivation is not anchored in the spectators.

Setting up the arrival will take some explaining. Sophocles wants to get the causal chain rolling quickly, so he starts with something smaller and simpler. He lets a group of children, young men and priests invade Oedipus' yard praying. Their appearance is a likely consequence of the circumstantial knot. Oedipus decides he wants to talk to them himself. The chain is rolling.

A handful of lines of verse, that is all Sophocles needs to set up the first motivation. Actually, it is already set up even before. When the priest sits on the stage and Oedipus sees him, this motivates Oedipus to walk over.

One could compare this gradual build up to *Iphigenia among the Taurians*, where Iphigenia walks on stage and explains the knot directly to the spectators.

Now let's look at how Sophocles keeps the chain going.

Oedipus turns to the priest. "Priest of Zeus, we respect your age, your high office. / Speak. / Why are you kneeling? Are you afraid, old man? / What can I give you? / How can I help? Ask. / Ask me anything. Anything at all. / My heart would be stone / if I felt no pity for these poor shattered people of mine / kneeling here at my feet."

Oedipus' address changes the situation. The initiative is turned over to the priest, who now has motivation to speak.

The priest stands up and bows. "Oedipus, lord of Thebes, you see us," he points towards the children and young men, "the people of Thebes, your people, / crowding in prayer around your altar, these small children here, old men bent with age, priests, and I, the priest of Zeus, and our noblest young men, the pride and strength of Thebes. / (...) / Look, / look at it, / lord Oedipus- right there, / in front of your eyes — this city- / it reels under a wild storm of blood, wave after wave battering Thebes. / (...) / We hunger, our world shivers with hunger. A disease hungers, nothing grows, wheat, fruit, nothing grows bigger than a seed. / Our women bear / dead things, / all they can do is grieve, / our cattle wither, stumble, drop to the ground, / flies simmer on their bloated tongues, / the plague spread everywhere, a stain seeping through our streets, our fields, our house, / look — god's fire eating everyone, everything, / (....) / Help us. Oedipus, we beg you, we all turn to you, kneeling to your greatness. / (...)"

The nature of the knot is revealed. We learn that a plague is ravaging Thebes, the city is about to go under, and Oedipus is the only one who can save it. The stakes are set high. The suffering is already there, and the threat is that it will not go away. It is clear to us that the knot will not be solved easily.

At the same time, a motivation for Oedipus to answer is set up. He does. His response is triggered by the immediate stimuli, but the response itself reflects his character and his understanding of the knot. The effect of his speech is to reveal more of the knot.

OEDIPUS: (...) / You have not wakened me from some kind of sleep. / I have wept, struggled, wandered in this maze of thought, / (...) / I sent my wife's brother, Creon, to great Apollo's shrine at Delphi; / I set him to learn what I must say or do to save Thebes, / But his long absence troubles me. Why isn't he here? Where is he? / (...) (Berg-Clay, 88-94)

This is how causality in *King Oedipus* works. Actions spring out of both an immediate stimulus and the inner logic of the situation as a whole. Each action modifies the situation by throwing new light on it or transforming the character or the knot. The altered situation contains stimulus that motivates the next action.

The initiative is thrown back and forth between Oedipus and the knot, creating an action-reaction chain. Both respond and act according to their own character.

We just learned who Oedipus is waiting for and why. Strictly speaking, it is back story. It would have been chronologically correct to say this before. But Sophocles thinks the correct place in the plot is here when the motivation for sending him has been anchored in the spectators. First the motivation to send him had to be set up. Then we were allowed to learn that he was already sent. Now that we know this, Sophocles allows him to arrive.

The priest looks towards the left stage entrance. "You speak of Creon, and Creon is here."

54

Making the sending of Creon into back story is a trick Sophocles uses to compress the plot. By doing this he avoids wasting story time on waiting for Creon's return, which makes it easier to conform to the genre convention of keeping the plot inside one revolution of the sun.

But breaking chronology to put it here is a statement as well. The correct place for an action to be revealed to the spectator is when the motivation has been revealed to them. For Sophocles, the plot is spectator centric, not character centric.

Nothing is allowed to happen in the plot before a stimulus is anchored in the spectators.

At one point in the story, a messenger comes from Corinth with news about the death of Oedipus' adoptive father. The cause of the death is unrelated to the plot, and one would think it impossible for Sophocles to invent a stimulus triggering the arrival of the messenger.

JOCASTA: Lords of Thebes, I come to the temples of the god / with offerings — this incense and this branch. / So many thoughts torture Oedipus. He never rests. / (...) / I have tried to reassure him, but nothing helps. / So I have come to you — ˙/ Apollo, close to my life, close to this house, / listen to my prayers: (she kneels) help us purify ourselves of this disease, / help us survive the long night of our suffering, / protect us. We are afraid when we see Oedipus confused / and frightened — Oedipus the only man who can pilot Thebes / to safety.

(Berg-Clay, 1159-1174)

The messenger arrives immediately after this, in response to Jocasta's prayers. One may argue about whether this arrival is a necessary or likely consequence of the prayer, as Aristotle requires, but it shows exactly how unwilling Sophocles is to compromise on the causal chain.

For a story to flow well, every action needs an immediate, or almost immediate, motivation. If it lacks one, the inner movie of the spectator becomes jerky. Epic poems, like the *Iliad* of Homer, may have causal chains that are halted when jumping back and forth between plot lines. In a story like *King Oedipus*, which has only one chain, it becomes almost completely linear. The effects of each action and episode set up the next.

Sometimes, especially with surprise twists, more than one cause is active. These can be a character trait that the spectators have been made aware of earlier, like when Oedipus infers that Creon and Tiresias conspire against him. Or they can be an action that is initiated but will not be completed until later, like the arrival of the shepherd that Oedipus asked Jocasta to send for.

The causal chain dies naturally when the last threat is resolved, for either a happy or unhappy outcome, and loose threads are collected.

Characters to Root For

The most important thing for characters in a suspense genre, like the Greek tragedy, is that we care and root for them.

This is why Aristotle in the *Poetics* says that the tragedy, unlike the comedy, should have persons that are better than us. We should perceive them as good.

Moral character is revealed by choices. One way of arranging this is by presenting the person with a dilemma. In *Iphigenia among the Taurians* there is an instructive example. The travel companion of Orestes is about to be sacrificed, but Orestes insists on taking his place. This self-sacrifice instantly makes us root for him.

That the character should be good does not mean that they must be perfect. When a negative trait is necessary for the plot, it is okay for the character to have it, as long as they, like the stubborn Achilles in the *Iliad*, are good in other respects. They should not be more flawed than they need to be.

Good can mean well-intentioned. In *King Oedipus* the play starts by Oedipus showing compassion for his people. He promises that he will free the city of the plague and puts action behind his words. This compassion makes us forgive his rash nature.

Later on, he accuses his brother-in-law of treason. Creon is innocent, so this, of course, is not a just act. But as Oedipus has reason to believe what he believes, we perceive the action as justifiable. A king has a right to protect himself from usurpers, and although his suspicion is mistaken, we see that his motive is self-defense.

Another way of evoking empathy is through undeserved misfortune. Aristotle mentions this as causing pity, but pity is closely related to empathy. Where a great and imminent misfortune evokes pity, lesser and more distant misfortune evokes empathy. In *King Oedipus*, we root for the three-day-old baby that had his feet pierced together to be put out to die. In *Iphigenia*, we root for Orestes after his unselfish act partly because of the price he is willing to pay. It was not fair that his friend should die, but it was also not fair that Orestes should. Our moral sense makes us root for someone we perceive as treated unfairly.

Deserved misfortune will not make us sympathize with the character in the same way. The moral instinct is that wickedness should be punished. So for this to work, it is important that the character is perceived as good.

Apart from being good, the character should be appropriate to who they are. It would seem wrong if a woman acted like a man, a beggar like a king, or a land crab like a sailor. People are formed by their environment and by expectations.

Next, the persons should behave in ways that are plausible according to their character. In the beginning of *King Oedipus*, Sophocles plants the traits that affect the important decisions of Oedipus later. Oedipus' tendency to see conspiracies, his rashness, and his insistence on discovering the truth are all established early. This means that the spectators can identify them as a cause, at least on an unconscious level, later on when he accuses Creon of conspiracy, strikes back at his father in anger, or insists on learning the truth about his parents.

The principle of necessary or probable consequence, and perhaps the cryptic requirement that characters should be *like* (like what?), implies that the poet should know something about psychology. In his *Rhetorics* Aristotle mentions seven causes of action: chance, nature, compulsion, habit, reason, anger, and desire. These are worth looking into. But what causes the causes? The tragedy shows the persons trying to untie a circumstantial knot, and they mutually affect each other. According to what laws?

Finally, the character should be consistent. If inconsistent, they should be consistently inconsistent. If a choice in the beginning of the play reveals one set of moral values, one should not have the character make the opposite choice in the ending— unless what happened between made the change plausible, that is.

Aristotle's Poetics

1 (47a8) – Mimetic Means

[1447a8] On poetry itself, its kinds and the powers of each, including how to construct the plot (10) of a good poem, the number and nature of the elements, and other topics relevant to the subject. Let us begin, as is natural, with the basics.

Epic and tragic poetry, as well as comedy and dithyrambic poetry, and most kinds of music played on wind or string instruments are mimetic arts. They differ in three respects; by the means, the subjects, and the ways.

Some can, (20) through craft or experience, imitate[1] with colors and shapes, and create the likeness of many things. Others do so with voice. In

---

[1] Modern English terms have not evolved to capture the characteristics of the mimesis that are important in Aristotle's model. Sculpture and painting are analogous to the tragedy in that they require an understanding of anatomy where the tragedy requires an understanding of psychology. Yet, emulation will not work as translation for mimesis when referring to them.

the arts mentioned above the emulation (*mimesis*) is done with rhythm, language, or melody, either separately or in combination.

In music played on a flute (*aulos*) or a lyre (*kithara*), only melody and rhythm are used. The same is true for other, similar arts, like playing the pan pipe. Dancers use rhythm without melody. Dance emulates character, circumstance, and action through poses and rhythmic movement[2].

The mimetic arts that use only language, whether in prose or in pure or mixed metric form, **[1447b]** remain unnamed. We have no term that gives a common name to the fables of Sophron and Xenarchus and the Socratic dialogues. Neither is there one for emulations put in iambic trimeter, elegiac couplets, or similar. The word *poet* is associated with the verse form, (10) we speak of *elegiac poets* and *epic poets* not based on whether they emulate, but on their use of verse. Someone who puts a treatise on medicine in verse is called a poet.

But Homer and Empedocles have nothing in common except the verse form. The first is rightly called a poet, (20) while the second should be called

---

[2]Character, circumstance, action and mimetic form come back in the four types of tragedies listed in *Poetics* 18 (Janko, 1987). They are probably the four parts of tragedy mentioned in the passing there. See also the discussion of the *Iliad* and *Odyssey* in *Poetics* 24. Bywater (1909) sees *praxis* and *pathos* as *what you do and what is done to you*. The greek word *pathos* means both *circumstance* and *emotion*. In the context of the *Poetics* I interpret it as *emotionally charged situation* and sometimes *traumatic situation*.

a natural scientist and not a poet. Someone who emulates in a mix of verse forms, like Chaermon did with his *Centaur*, should also be called a poet. This is how we shall define this.

Some arts use all the mentioned means; rhythm, language, and melody. These include the chorally performed dithyrambs and nomes, and comedies and tragedies. The former use all the three means throughout, while the latter use different ones in different parts.

This is how the arts differ by use of mimetic means.

2 (48a1) – Mimetic Subject

[1448a] The subjects of emulation are those doing things. These must be serious-and-good (*spoudaious*) or petty-and-mean (*phaulous*), as this is our main way of characterizing people based on their defects (*kakia*) and qualities (*arete*). It follows that they must be better than, worse than or as ourselves.

The same is true in painting. Polygnotus used to paint better persons, Pauson worse ones, and Dionysius those like us. This applies to all the mimetic arts we have mentioned, and it is how they differ by subject. We find it even in dance, flute and (10) lyre play, as well as in prose and naked verse. Homer emulated better persons. Cleophon those like us. Hegemon of Thasos, who invented parodies, and Nicochares, who wrote the *Deiliad*, emulated worse. Dithyrambs and nomes take different

62

moral types as their subjects as well; Timotheus and Philoxenus differed in how they emulated the cyclops.

It is in this respect that tragedy and comedy differ. Comedy tends to emulate persons worse than us, and tragedy those better than us.

3 (48a18) – Mimetic Ways

The way in which the subjects are emulated is a third difference. (20) By the same means, the same subject can be emulated through narration—in this case, the poet can either become another, as Homer does, or speak as himself, unchanged—or the emulation can be acted out in front of us.

These are the three respects that we pointed out in the beginning, in which the mimetic arts differ; the means, the subjects, and the ways.

In one respect, Sophocles emulates like Homer, as both have better persons as their subjects. In another, he emulates like Aristophanes, as both have the emulation acted out (*drontas*). (30)

Some say this is why we call it *drama*, on which the Dorians base the claim that they invented the tragedy and comedy. The Megarians make the claim to comedy; not only those of mainland Greece, who say that it originated under their democracy, but those of Sicily as well. The poet Epicharmus, whose time was much earlier than that of Chionides and Magnes, came from there. Tragedy is claimed by certain Pelopponese Dorians.

When arguing for this, they point to language.

They call villages *komai*, while the Athenians call them *demoi*, and they claim that the comedians got their name not from their reveling (*komazein*), but from going from village to village, as they were chased in disgrace from the city. **[1448b]** They also point out that their term for doing is *dran*, while the Athenians call it *prattein*.

This is enough on the number and types of differences in emulations.

4 (48b4) – The Birth of Drama

Poetry most likely sprung from two causes, both of human nature.

Emulation is natural to us from childhood. Humans differ from other living creatures in having a stronger inclination towards emulation, and in taking their first steps of learning through it.

Additionally, we all find pleasure in the mimetic. This is revealed by (10) our fascination for watching life-like imitations of things that repel us when we see them in life, like disgusting animals or dead bodies. The reason for this is that figuring something out is enjoyable, not only to philosophers but to everyone, even though most do it to a lesser extent. They enjoy watching a picture and figure out who, for example, this or that person is. If one has never seen what is imitated before, the pleasure is derived from studying the craft, the colors, or something else. (20)

Like emulation, melody and rhythm are natural to us. Meter is obviously rhythmic. People with natural inclinations towards these things exercised their talent, and poetry evolved from their improvisations. Next, it evolved in two directions, reflecting the dispositions of the poets. The serious emulated the serious actions of better persons. The playful emulated the actions of lesser persons. The latter composed satires at first, while the former made hymns to the gods and praises to famous men.

We do not have any satirical poem predating Homer, but there were probably many. Beginning with Homer, we can cite numerous, (30) like his own *Margites* and similar poems. The best meters for such poems were found at about this time. The verse form is still called iambic, being the one in which people wrote lampoons (*iamboi*) against one another, so the poets composed in heroic or lampoonic verse.

Homer is preeminent in the serious style. He is the only one who mastered both the poetic form and the emulation. But he also laid the foundation for comedy by dramatizing the ridiculous instead of the vindictive. His *Margites* stand in the same relation to comedy as the *Iliad* and the *Odyssey* do to tragedy.

[1449a] When the tragedy and comedy arrived, the poets continued to follow their respective inclinations. Comedy was pursued in place of lampoons, tragedy in place of epic poems, as drama was a more popular and higher art form.

Whether tragedy has yet found its form or not,

in itself or in relation to the spectators, is another topic.

At first, (10) tragedy and comedy were improvised. The first evolved from the dithyramb, the second from the phallic songs that live on in many cities. Tragedy evolved in steps, with each new technique being developed as it was discovered. Having gone through many iterations, it found its form and stabilized.

Aeschylus introduced a second actor. He also reduced the importance of the chorus and put dialogue in the center. Sophocles raised the number of actors to three and added stage painting.

Concerning magnitude, it was not until late that the light plots and (20) diction inherited from the satyric origins were discarded for heavier ones. The trochaic tetrameter, associated with the satyric and with dance, was replaced with the iambic meter, which, once dialogue entered, revealed itself to be the right choice. Of all meters, the iambic is the one resembling speech the most. We see this in everyday speech, where we often use iambic, but rarely hexameter, and when we do, it is only in a tone that is not conversational.

How the number of episodes and other parts (30) are said to have evolved must be taken as is. To discuss them in detail would be a large undertaking.

5 (49a32) – Comedy and Epic Poetry

Comedy is, as we said, an emulation of lesser persons. However, not in the sense of evil. The laughable is a type of ugly. It consists of a defect or ugliness that is not painful or destructive. An obvious example is the comic mask, which is ugly and distorted but does not convey pain.

The evolutionary steps of the tragedy, and who was behind these changes, are well known. Comedy has no history, as it was not taken seriously at first. **[1449b]** The magistrate granted the poets a comic chorus late, and until then they were volunteers. Comedy had already found its form before we hear of comic poets. We do not know who introduced masks and prologues, increased the number of actors, and such.

The comic plot originally came from Sicily. The Athenian poet Crates was the first who, dropping the parodic form, generalized themes and plots.

Epic poetry is similar to tragedy (10) in that it is an emulation of serious-and-good persons in verse. They differ in that epic poetry always uses the same meter and is narrated. They also differ in length. The tragedy tries, as much as possible, to stay inside a single revolution of the sun, or to exceed this only slightly, while the epic plot has no time constraint. So this is a difference, though at first, the tragedy had the same freedom as epic poetry.

When it comes to the elements, some are common to both, some are specific to the tragedy. Anyone who knows what a good or bad tragedy is can also judge epic poetry. All the elements of an epic poem are found in tragedy, but not all the elements of the tragedy are found in an (20) epic poem.

6 (49b21) – Defining Tragedy

We will talk about epic poetry[3] and comedy later. Let us now discuss the tragedy, starting with its formal definition based on what has been said.

Tragedy is an emulation (*mimesis*) of an action (*praxis*) that is serious-and-good (*spoudaios*), complete (*teleios*), and of a certain magnitude (*megethos*); in garnished language, different kinds in different parts of the play; dramatized, not narrated[4]; evoking pity (*eleos*) and fear (*phobos*), and reaching the purgation (*katharsis*) of such emotions. By *garnished language*, I mean language with rhythm, musicality, and song. By *different kinds in different parts*, (30) I mean that some parts are rendered through verse alone, others with song.

As the emulation is performed by actors, it follows, first, that the stage show[5] (*opsis*) is a part of the tragedy and, next, that songs and language are, for these are the means of emulation. By *language*

---

[3]Really "mimesis in hexameter", which is the meter of epic poetry.

[4]This is obvious since the tragedy is staged and performed by actors. But even episodes that are related through messenger speeches are usually dramatized by the relater.

[5]*Opsis* really means appearance of a person or thing. Perhaps the most accurate in the context is just show, but as show is a common verb as well as a noun, I use stage show.

I mean metrically arranged words. The meaning of *songs* should be clear enough.

Tragedy is an emulation of an action, and it shows persons engaged in action. These must have character (*ethos*) and reason (*dianoia*), as it is by these that we assign traits to their actions, **[1450a]** and it is through these that they hit or miss the mark[6]. The emulated action we call plot (*muthos*), and by *plot* I mean the organization of the incidents (*pragmata*). By character I mean that which enables us to assign traits to the persons. Reason is required wherever a statement is proved or a general truth expressed.

It follows that every tragedy has six elements, namely, plot, character, language, (10) reason, stage show, and music. Two are the means (language and music), one the way (stage show), and three the subjects (plot, character, and reason) of emulation. This is the full list. These elements have been employed by all poets. In fact every play has stage show as well as character, plot, language, song, and reason.

The organization of the incidents is the most important element, as tragedy emulates not men, but action and life. The key to happiness and misery is action. Our aim is doing something, not being a type. People are a type because of their character, (20) but happy or not through their actions. The

---

[6]Following Howland (1995, pp. 377-378). Usually translated as succeed or fail. Possibly hit or miss the mark refers to the type of mistake (hamartia) discussed in chapter 13.

persons do not act with the aim of revealing character, but their actions reveal who they are. We can conclude that the incidents and the plot are the aim of the tragedy, and the aim is what matters most. Without action there cannot be a tragedy, but without defined character there can. Indeed, the tragedies of most of our modern poets do not render character well, and there are many such poets. It is the same in painting, and this is the difference between Zeuxis and Polygnotus. Polygnotus delineates character well; the style of Zeuxis is devoid of character.

Also, if you string together speeches that reveal character, have eloquent language, (30) and are well reasoned, you will not produce the essential tragic effect nearly so well as with a play which, however deficient in these respects, has a good plot and well-constructed incidents. Additionally, the most powerful techniques for evoking emotional interest, reversals and recognitions, belong to the plot. A further proof is that novices in the art master language and character before they can construct the plot. We see this with almost all inexperienced[7] poets.

So the plot is the central concept and soul of a tragedy, with character in second place. A similar observation can be made about painting. [1450b] Beautiful colors laid on randomly will not give as much pleasure as the chalk outline of a portrait.

_____

[7]Most translate *prôtoi* as *early*. This suggests poets from an earlier time. *Inexperienced* fits the context better.

The tragedy is the emulation of an action, and through this also of character.

Third is reason. That is, saying what is logical and relevant in the situation. In the case of speeches, this is a political and rhetorical art. Earlier poets made their characters speak like political leaders; the poets of our time like orators. As character is revealed by the choices a person makes, it is not revealed (10) by speeches where nothing is chosen or avoided. Reason, on the other hand, is found if anything is proven to be or not to be, or if a general idea is expressed.

Fourth is language, by which I mean, as already mentioned, expression of meaning through words. This is the same in verse as in prose.

Of the remaining, song is the most important and it is also the most garnished.

The stage show can, indeed, evoke emotions, but it is the least artistic element, and it is not part of the poetic art. The tragedy has emotional impact even when not performed by actors in the festival competitions. (20) The stage show depends more on the stage production[8] than the art of the poet.

7 (50b21) – Causality

With these principles in place, let us discuss how the incidents should be organized, as this is what matters most in the tragedy.

---

[8]Usually translated as stage machinist or painter, but in reality there must have been costumes, masks, choreography as well as scenography and special effects.

According to our definition, tragedy is an emulation of an action that is complete, whole, and of a certain magnitude[9], as something can be whole and lack magnitude.

Whole is that which has a beginning, middle, and end. A *beginning* follows nothing by causal necessity, but leads to something else. An *end*, on the contrary, follows something, (30) by necessity or as a likely consequence, but has nothing following it. A *middle* follows something as it is followed by something else. A well constructed plot cannot begin or end at random, but must comply with these principles.

A beautiful object, whether it is a living organism or any whole composed of parts, should not only have its parts in the right place. It should also be of a certain magnitude, as beauty depends on magnitude as well as order. Too tiny an organism cannot be beautiful because we cannot clearly distinguish something that is visible for an imperceptible moment. Something too enormous cannot be beautiful because when the eye is unable to take the whole in, **[1451a]** the sense of unity is lost. Imagine a creature that is a thousand miles long. Like inanimate bodies and organisms, which should have a magnitude that enable us to take them in, the plot should have adequate length. One that can easily be held in memory.

---

[9]Seems to refer to the size-and-weight of the knot, or the complexity and stakes of the story problem, which indirectly affect the length of the tragedy.

The limitation in length imposed by the competitions on shows[10] is not part of the art. Had the format been that a hundred tragedies should compete, the performance would be timed against the water-clock, as is proposed now and then[11]. (10) The limit implied by the tragedy itself is that greater magnitude is better, as long as we can take in the whole. Stated simply, the magnitude is adequate when an arc from a bad situation to a good or a good situation to a bad can be completed through logically connected steps.

8 (51a16) – Unity

The plot is not unified, as some think, just by being about one person. An infinite number of things happen in a person's life without making them a unity. The many actions of one person will not make up a single action[12]. (20)

---

[10]Really "perceptions," like in "performances and the perception [of them]" (Janko, 1987), but it does not make sense in the context.

[11]Literally "as they say now and then". It sounds like a proposition that could come up after extra long and boring plays. Taràn (2012) has "as people at some other times say they compete" where *other times* refer to speeches in court, but Aristotle would know of this practice and not quote others. Sachs (2005) has "as people claim they did at some time or other", but there is no evidence of such a practice, and it seems like a bad idea to cheat the audience of the ending. Janko (1987) has "as the saying goes".

[12]In the beginning of the *Nicomachean Ethics* (1094a8) Aristotle observes that the end of a subordinate activity can be the means towards the end of a master activity. In this way many lesser actions can make up a higher, single action, by

Poets who compose a *Heraclid*, a *Theseid*, and other poems of the kind make this mistake. They think that as Heracles is one man, the story of Heracles will make up a unity. But Homer, who excels in so many respects, gets—through craft or instinct—this right as well. In the *Odyssey*, he did not include everything that happened to Odysseus. Incidents such as his wound on Parnassus or his pretended madness during the conscription are left out. Even if one thing happened it is not necessarily the cause of another. In the *Odyssey*, Homer included only what makes up a single action in our sense, and the same goes for the (30) *Iliad*.

Like in other mimetic arts where the imitation is one when the subject is one, the plot, which emulates an action, has to emulate an action that is one and whole. The structure should be such that if any one part is displaced or removed, the whole is disjointed and disturbed. If the presence or absence of something makes no visible difference, it is not an organic part of the whole.

9 (51a36) – Universals

It is clear from what has been said that it is not the task of the poet to show what has happened, but what could happen (according to the laws of probability or necessity)[13]. The difference between the poet and the historian is not that they write

---

contributing towards the same higher end.

[13]This indicates that tragic mimesis is emulation or simulation rather than representation or imitiation.

verse or prose. **[1451b]** The work of Herodotus could be put into verse, and it would still be history, whether the form is metrical or not. The real difference is that one relates what has happened, while the other relates what could happen. Poetry is, in consequence, more philosophical and higher than history. Poetry shows the universal; history shows the specific. By the universal, I mean how the things a person does or says in a situation are governed by the laws of probability and necessity. This universality is what (10) poetry strives for, even though it assigns historical[14] names to the persons. The specific is, for example, what Alcibiades did or suffered.

In comedy this is obvious. Here the poet first constructs a probable plot, and then assigns names. In this they differ from the lampooners who write about specific individuals. Tragedians use real names to add credibility. What has not happened we cannot be sure is possible, but what has happened evidently is, or it would not have happened. Still some tragedies have only one (20) or two well known names, the rest being fictitious. In others, none are well known, as in Agathon's *Antheus*, where both incidents and names are fictitious. Yet they are no less enjoyable.

We do not, therefore, have to keep to received legends at all costs, even if they usually are the

---

[14]Not explicit, but clear from the context. Aristotle is arguing that the use of myths, which were then considered historical sources, does not make tragedies history.

subject of tragedy. Indeed, it would be absurd to attempt it. Even the known are known only to a few, but are still enjoyable to all.

It follows that the poet is a creator of plots rather than verses. He is a poet because he creates emulations, and what is emulated are actions. Even if he happens $_{(30)}$ to take on a historical subject, he can still be a poet, as there is no reason why events that have happened could not conform to laws of probability and necessity. Creating the causality makes him a poet.

Of all plots and actions, the episodic are the worst. I call a plot *episodic* when the episodes do not follow one another through probable or necessary consequence. Bad poets compose such pieces because of themselves, while good poets stretch the plot beyond its capacity to impress the competition judges[15], often forcing them to break the natural continuity.

[1452a] But tragedy is an emulation of not only an action that is complete but one that evokes fear and pity as well. This can be effectively achieved through something unexpected that is at the same time a logical consequence. This makes a stronger impression than if it happened by itself and by coincidence. Even coincidences have greater impact when they seem to happen for a reason. For instance the statue of Mitys at Argos, which fell upon and killed Mity's murderer, who was looking at

---

[15]Following Hubbard (1972). Most say "because of the actors."

it. Such events seem to not (10) happen by chance.
Plots constructed in this way are therefore better.

10 (52a12) – Simple and Twisted Plots

Plots are either simple or twisted[16], like the
actions that they emulate. By simple action I mean
one which is continuous and unchanging and has
an arc[17] (*metabasis*) without reversals (*peripeteia*)
and recognitions (*anagnorisis*).

A twisted action has an arc with reversals, recognitions or both. These should arise from the plot
structure as (20) a necessary or probable consequence of what has preceded. It makes a big difference whether an event is caused by something or
just follows it.

---

[16]*Twisted* as in twisted rope is a more literal translation
than *complex*, which is normally preferred.

[17]Literally "change". The arc at any time either moves away
from a bad situation towards a better one or from a better
towards a worse one. If the arc always moves in the same
direction, Aristotle calls the plot simple; if it is twisting and
turning, the plot is twisted. Flipping the arc is discussed in
the next chapter. How to set up a negative arc is the subject
of chapter 13. The length of the arc is discussed in chapter
18. At the end of chapter 7 Aritotle speaks of a completed arc
or transition, which is not quite the same as the prospective
change of the arc.

11 (52a22) – Reversal, Recognition and Circumstance

A reversal flips the arc of the events towards the opposite[18] while complying with the principles of probable or necessary consequence in the way mentioned. Like in *Oedipus*, where the messenger comes to cheer Oedipus and free him from his fears about his mother, but reveals the opposite[19]. Or as in *Lynceus*, where Lynceus is led away to his death, and Danaus goes with him, meaning to kill him. But as a consequence of what has happened before, Danaus is killed and Lynceus saved.

Recognition, (30) as the name indicates, is a change from ignorance to knowledge, for example, leading to friendship or enmity between characters the poet has set up an arc for[20]. A recognition is most effective when it triggers a reversal, like in

---

[18]Following Else (1957) who argues that opposite means the opposite type of fortune.

[19]Oedipus does not want to return to Corinth because it is prophecied that he will share a bed with his mother. The messenger tells Oedipus that Merope is not his real mother, but that a shepherd from the household of Laius was supposed to put him out to die. This is enough to make his wife Jocasta (and the spectators, if they did not know already) recognize that Oedipus is really her son. Janko (1987) also reached the conclusion that this passage speaks of Jocasta's recognition. This recognition flips the arc that was headed towards a positive discovery (that the prophecies cannot be fulfilled) to head towards a negative discovery (that they already are). Jocasta and the spectators see this coming, but Oedipus misjudges her reaction and continues to pursue the truth. This way of setting up a negative arc through a mistake or misjudgement is discussed in chapter 13.

[20]Meaning character we are supposed to root for or against.

Oedipus[21]. There are other types of recognition as well. Even trivial objects may be the subject of a recognition, and we could recognize whether a person has done or not done something. But the kind of recognition best serving the purpose of the plot is the one above. This kind of recognition, when it leads to a reversal, evokes pity or fear, **[1452b]** which, by definition, is what the tragedy tries to do. Moreover, a better or worse situation results from such a moment.[22]

As this kind of recognition is between persons, it is possible that only one is recognized by the other, if it becomes clear who one of them is. Or they both may recognize each other. Iphigenia is recognized by Orestes by the sending of the letter, but another recognition is required to make Orestes known to Iphigenia.

Reversal and recognition are two plot components. (10) A third is circumstance[23] (*pathos*). The circumstance is a destructive or painful act, with a revealed threat[24] of death, bodily agony, wounds

---

[21]King Oedipus has many recognitions and reversals, but Aristotle must refer to the example given above, where Jocasta recognizes the true identity of Oedipus.

[22]These points apply to plots that set one friend or family member against another because of a mistake, which is Aristotle's preferred plot type for tragedies. This plot type is the subject of chapters 13 and 14.

[23]Usually translated as suffering. The dictionary translates *pathos* as emotion or circumstance. The Poetics uses it in the sense of a violent climax, but tragedies often have motivational *pathos* as well.

[24]Janko (1987) translates *phanero* to "deaths in full view" and comments that it is often translated to "deaths on the

and the like.

12 (52b14) – Sections

The defining elements of the tragedy have been discussed already. Let us now look at the sections it is divided into. These are the prologue (*prologos*), episode (*epeisodion*), exit (*exodos*) and choral parts, of which the processional (*parodos*) and stationary (*stasimon*) are always used. Some can additionally have songs by actors on the stage and dirges (*kommos*).

The prologue is an acted part that comes before the [20] processional. Episodes come between choral parts. The exit is an acted part that comes after the last choral.

Of the choral parts, the processional is the first song by the chorus alone. A stationary is a song by the chorus without anapestic or trochaic verse. And a dirge is a lament involving both chorus and actors.

The defining elements of the tragedy were discussed previously. Here we listed the sections the tragedy is divided into.

---

stage." He notes, however, that such events in Greek tragedies are usually narrated in messenger-speeches, so this does not really make sense. Tragedies use danger and threats to set the stakes and to create tension and evoke fear. For this to work, the threat has to be made explicit to the spectators, and I have assumed this is the point Aristotle wants to make. Schmitt (2008) translates it to "bekannt" ("known").

13 (52b28) – Intent and Arc

In continuation of what has been said, we will discuss what the poet should strive for, and what he should avoid, when constructing plots. We will also address how the effects that are characteristic (30) to the tragedy are achieved.

As we have seen, the ideal tragedy should not have a simple, but a twisted plot. It should, moreover, emulate an action that evokes pity and fear, as this is what makes it tragic.

It follows, first, that the intention of the action[25] cannot be to throw decent men from a good situation to a bad, as this arouses neither pity nor fear. It is merely repulsive[26]. Nor should it be to move a wicked man from a bad situation to a good. Nothing is less tragic; it has not a single tragic quality. It neither evokes sympathy[27] (*philantropos*) nor pity or fear. **[1453a]** Nor should the downfall of a wholly despicable man be the intent. A plot with

---

[25]Implicit. The change towards worse must have a cause. This cause is the active and visible intention of the plot. Other interpretations lead to logical inconsistencies.

[26]This has confused many commentators who have interpreted Aristotle to say that we will not have empathy with a good person falling into misfortune. Aristotle's point, however, is that we cannot sympathize with an action with this intention. In chapter 14 he mentions Medea deciding to kill her children in Euripides' play as an example of this plot type. The abusive actions of the suitors in the Odyssey are repulsive in this sense.

[27]While pity (*eleos*) is evoked by undeserved misfortune, sympathy (*philantropos*) seems to be evoked by deserved escape from misfortune. *Goodwill* or *support* are translations.

this intention evokes sympathy[28], but it inspires neither pity nor fear. Pity is aroused by undeserved misfortune, and fear by danger against someone we identify with[29]. So this plot is neither suspenseful nor heart-wrenching.

What remains is the case between, where someone is thrown[30] towards misfortune not by (acts of) unusual quality and justness or defects and wickedness[31], but because of $_{(10)}$ a mistake[32] (*hamartia*). This should happen to someone who is renowned and prosperous[33], like Oedipus, Thyestes, or other men of such families.

A well-constructed plot should, therefore, have a single interest, rather than, as some advocate, a

---

[28]It is possible that Aristotle considers this plot (stopping evil) to be identical to the one left out (saving someone good from evil), which would explain why it evokes sympathy.

[29]Usually "like us." Aristotle seems headed for the opposite of "despicable," which would be someone we like. In the *Rethorics* Aristotle says that fear is "for ourselves," which would imply "someone we identify with" or "care for as they were our own."

[30]Following Malcolm Heath (2017, section 6), who argues for interpreting this change as a trajectory, and not as a completed change.

[31]Implying an action that intends to stop a wicked person or harm someone innocent. The usual interpretation that the person should not be brought down by his own character causes logical problems. Aristotle argues against plots centered around a good hero fighting a villain or a villain harming someone innocent, like Odysseus or the suitors in the Odyssey.

[32]For this arc to work, the spectators must be aware of the mistake, so it implies dramatic irony. If the misfortune is undeserved, it will evoke pitiful fear in the spectators who will want to see the mistake averted.

[33]This will make the threatened fall seem more dramatic.

double interest knot[34]. The arc should not be from bad towards good, but the other way—from good towards bad. It should not be caused by wickedness[35] but by a mistake made by a character as just described, or someone better rather than worse[36].

The practice of the stage confirms this view. At first, the poets adapted any legend. Now, the best tragedies are founded on the stories of a few houses, (20) on the fates of Alcmaeon, Oedipus, Orestes, Meleager, Thyestes, Telephus, and others who have suffered or caused a traumatic circumstance.

The ideal tragedy, then, should be constructed like this. Those who criticise Euripides for doing this[37] or even for letting many plays end unhappily are wrong because it is, as we have shown, correct. The best proof is that when performed in dramatic competitions, such plays, if staged well, are the most tragic. Euripides, in spite of his other flaws, (30) is perceived to be the most tragic of the poets.

The second best way, which some put first, is to build the plot around a double interest knot, like the *Odyssey* which has opposite outcomes for the

---

[34]Really single and double structure (Janko, 1987). The point Aristotle is making is that the ideal tragic plot should revolve around the mistake, and not around the opposing interests of two sides.

[35]Having a wicked side set up a trap, like the suitors do for Telemachus in the *Odyssey*, does not quite work in the same way. The spectators hope that Telemachus will outwit the suitors, rather than pity him.

[36]It is important that we can sympathize with the character.

[37]Having plots that set up a negative arc with a mistake and dramatic irony.

good and bad. It is considered the best because of the weakness of theatre audiences; the poets want to please the spectators. The pleasure, however, is not truly tragic. It is more in the spirit of comedy, where those who are deadly enemies in the play, like Orestes and Aegisthus, can walk off the stage as friends, and no one kills or is killed.

14 (53b1) – Knot and Resolution

[1453b] Fear and pity may be evoked by the stage show, but preferably they should be evoked by the plot, which is more difficult. The plot should be constructed so that even without seeing the things take place, he who hears the story should be filled with horror and pity,[38] as someone may be when hearing Oedipus.

To achieve impact through the stage show alone is less artistic, and a matter of stage production. Those who create a sense not of the terrifying but of the monstrous through stage effects (10) have misunderstood the purpose of tragedy. We should not ask from tragedy any kind of pleasure except those that belong to it.

Since the poet should evoke the pleasures of pity and fear through the emulation, the incidents should evoke such emotions. So let us discuss what kinds of incidents evoke fear in us or make us pity someone. It must be between persons who are

---

[38]Aristotle makes the point that the plot should stand on its own legs. It should make an impact even when the stage show is removed.

friends, enemies or indifferent to one another. If an enemy kills an enemy, there is nothing to excite pity[39] neither in the act nor the intention, except if the circumstance is dreadful and pitiful in itself. The same goes for people who are indifferent to each other.

But when the [20] circumstance occurs between two people who are near and dear to one another—if, for example, a brother stands against his brother, a son against his father, a mother against her son, a son against his mother—and one kills or almost kills the other, or does something similar, these are the situations to look for.

The poet cannot disregard the outcome of the original story, for instance, that Clytemnestra was killed by Orestes and Eriphyle by Alcmaeon. But he should be creative and handle the traditional material well. Let us be more clear about what is meant by *well*.

One can build up to a moment[40] where the act is committed consciously and in knowledge, in the way of earlier poets. Euripides makes Medea kill her children in this way.[41] Or where [30] the act

---

[39]The focus on pity and intention indicates that Aristotle is explaining how to construct the hamartia-plot. Killing an enemy because of a mistake does not evoke pity. Killing or intending to kill a friend because of a mistake does. Intending to kill a friend in knowledge is repulsive.

[40]The violence that was committed, or almost committed, in these families is used to set stakes and build anticipation of a traumatic climax.

[41]The Arabic, but none of the Greek, has: "Or they may be going to act, in full knowledge, but to not do it." (Janko,

has already been committed, but in ignorance, and the friendship or kinship is about to be recognized. Sophocles does this in *Oedipus*. Here the act is committed outside the plot, in the back story, but there are cases where it falls within. One could mention Astydamas' *Alcmaeon* or Telegonus in *Wounded Odysseus*. The third case is where someone is about to carry out the irreversible act in ignorance, but recognizes it before it is done.

These are the only possible ways for it must be carried out or not, and either in knowledge or in ignorance.

To be about to act in knowledge and then end up not doing it is the worst. The intent is repulsive[42] and the situation untragic, as there is no traumatic circumstance. This is why it never, or very rarely, is used. **[1454a]** One instance is in *Antigone*, where Haemon threatens Creon.

Next is that the act is carried out.

Even better, that the irreversible act is committed in ignorance, and the recognition happens later. In this case, the intent is not repulsive[43], while the

---

1987). The point of Aristotle, however, is to show how the irreversible act mentioned in the paragraph before and in chapter 13 can be used to create a climax. It is not possible to create a climactic moment if the hero does not show up. So it is likely that the omission is deliberate. There is a similar omission in chapter 13, where Aristotle does not mention the obvious, that an arc towards good for a good person is not tragic. Tarán (2012) holds a similar view.

[42]This points back to the repulsive intention of bringing decent persons to misfortune in chapter 13. The point also applies to the next step.

[43]We can sympathize because the person is making a mis-

recognition has a startling effect.

The last case is the best, like in *Cresphontes* when Merope is about to kill her son, but, recognizing who he is, spares his life. In *Iphigenia* the same happens; the sister recognizes the brother just in time[44]. In *Helle*, the son recognizes the mother when on the verge of giving her up.

This moment is the reason why only a few (10) families furnish the tragedies. The poets sought the tragic effect for some time, and it was not through forethought, but by trial and error that they discovered this technique. In time they became inclined to base their plays on the houses with stories that contain such traumatic circumstances.

This is enough on the organization of the incidents and on the best kind of plot.

15 (54a16) - Character

When it comes to character, there are four things to strive for.

First, and most important, the character should be resourceful-and-good[45] (*chresta*). A speech or

---

take.

[44]In the Iphigenia of Euripides, this is not the final climax. This indicates that Aristotle is discussing the build up of any climactic moment revolving around a traumatic situation, not only the end climax.

[45]Literally good-and-useful. This should not be read as good or bad inside an objective ethical system, but as our subjective reaction to people as cool guys that we can root for or uncool jerks we will root against. It is cool to have integrity and be a good friend. But it is also cool to be a clever fox like Odysseus and even cooler to outfox a clever jerk like Sisyphus.

action reveals character when choices are made. The character is resourceful-and-good if the choice is. This applies [20] to all classes. Even a woman or a slave can be resourceful-and- good, though the first class may be inferior and the second worthless.

Second, it should be appropriate. It is possible for a person to be brave, but it would seem out of character for a woman to be brave or clever in such a way.

Third is like[46]. This is different from good and appropriate.

Fourth, it should be consistent. If the emulated character type is inconsistent, the person must be consistently inconsistent.

An example of unnecessarily flawed character: The cowardice of Menelaus in *Orestes*. [30] Of the unsuitable or inappropriate: The lament of Odysseus in *Scylla*, and Melanippe's speech. Of inconsistency: *Iphigenia at Aulis*, where the begging Iphigenia in no way resembles her later self.

In character, as in the organization of the incidents, the poet should strive for the necessary or probable. A person with a certain character should speak or act in certain ways that are necessary or plausible for their character, in the same way that one incident should follow another through necessary or probable consequence.

---

[46]Usually interpreted as life-like or like us. The first could refer to the comparison to painting later in the chapter, the second to the point made about identification in chapter 13.

The untying should, obviously, happen through the plot, and not come about by *deus ex machina*, **[1454b]** like in *Medea* or in the return of the Greeks in the *Iliad*. The deus ex machina should only be used for things outside the plot—either things beyond human knowledge in the back story or something later that needs to be foretold, because we see the gods as able to know everything. In the plot itself, there should be nothing illogical. If something illogical cannot be avoided, it must be placed outside the plot, like in Sophocles' *Oedipus*[47].

Since the tragedy emulates persons that are better than us, poets should follow the example of good portrait painters. (10) They capture the distinctive features and create portraits that look like the model but are more beautiful. In the same way, the poet, when emulating someone ill-tempered, lazy, or morally lacking in other ways, should keep the trait and at the same time make their character good, like Homer does when he makes Achilles both stubborn and good.

These are the things the poet should look out for. Additionally we have the things that have to do with the stage show. There are many ways to go wrong here too, but enough has been said on this in my published work.

---

[47]Most improbable incidents in the back story of King Oedipus are there to prove that it is impossible to escape the prophecies. Fate finds a way to make it happen. So they are not defects. But Aristotle finds it unlikely that Oedipus had not heard how Laius was killed (Poetics, 24/60a29-32).

16 (54b19) – Kinds of Recognition

We have already explained what a recognition *is*. (20) Let us now take a closer look at the types.

The least artistic and, from lack of imagination, the one used most often is recognition by tokens. Some are present from birth, like the spear shaped birth-mark of the earth-born, or the star-shaped ones introduced by Carcinus in his *Thyestes*. Others are gotten after birth. Of these, some are bodily marks, like scars, and some are external tokens, like necklaces or the boat that caused the recognition in *Tyro*.

These can be handled more or less skillfully. The recognition of Odysseus by his scar is made in one way by the nurse, in another by the swineherd. The use of the token, or any type of recognition, just for confirmation is least artistic. Having it cause a reversal, like in the foot-washing scene with the nurse, is far better. (30)

Next are recognitions that are by the poet, which makes them inartistic. For example, in *Iphigenia* where Orestes says who he is. She is recognized through the letter, but he, when plainly saying who he is, is revealed by the poet and not through the plot. This has the same problem as the first type; Orestes might just as well have brought a token. A similar example is the voice of the weaving shuttle in Sophocles' *Tereus*.

The third type depends on memory. An association evokes emotion, **[1455b]** like in Dicaeogenes' *Cypriots*, where the hero breaks into tears upon seeing a picture. Or in the hall of Alcinous, where Odysseus, when listening to the lyre-player, is reminded of the past and weeps. This leads to recognition in both cases.

The fourth type happens through reasoning. In *Libation Bearers* we have this: Someone looking like me has arrived; no one but Orestes looks like me; therefore Orestes has arrived. In the sophist Polyidus' *Iphigenia*, it was natural for Orestes to say: 'So I too will die at the altar like my sister.'[48] In Theodectes' *Tydeus*, the father says: 'I came to find my son, and I lose my life.' (10) In the *Sons of Phineus* the women infer their fate when seeing the place. 'We will die here, for this is where the boys were cast out.'

There is also a type of recognition in combination with false inference. Like in Odysseus as false messenger. That he and no one else can string the bow is established by the poet. The assumption of the suitors said that Odysseus assessed the bow sent to him "because he never saw it before". By having the latter be recognized from the former the poet constructed a false inference.[49]

---

[48]This is mentioned in chapter 17. When Orestes says this, Iphigenia infers that he is her brother. This recognition by inference saves him.

[49]False recognitions are an important device. It is used in King Oedipus when Oedipus infers that Tiresias and Creon conspire, or when he infers that Jocasta is afraid that he is the son of poor parents. This use of recognition is worth pointing out, and it is probable that this is what Aristotle is doing here. The incident in Odyssey 21 referenced here fits the concept and roughly fits the phrases. The assumption that he has

But the best type of recognition is the one that arises from what has happened, where the startling recognition is a logical consequence like the one in Sophocles' *Oedipus*[50] and the one in *Iphigenia*, where it was logical that Iphigenia would want to send a letter. This is the only kind of recognition that does not depend on the [20] artificial help of tokens, such as amulets and the like. Second is recognitions through reasoning.

17 (55a22) – Creative Process

When composing the plot and putting it into words, the poet should visualize the scene as well as he can. By seeing everything vividly before him, as if he were present, he will discover what is in line with the action and be more unlikely to overlook inconsistencies.

The critique of Carcinus can serve as a warning. Amphiaraus stepped outside the sacred space. Someone not seeing it would miss this, but on stage it became obvious and the oversight offended the spectators.

As far as he can, the poet should work out the gestures[51]. [30] A poet is more convincing if he

---

never seen the bow serves as a false confirmation that the disguised beggar is not Odysseus. The passage is considered cryptic in the ancient Greek versions, and all translations are guesswork. The usual translation, which at least goes back to Bywater (1898), is obscure when read on its own, and very out of context. See for example Janko (1987).

[50]By Jocasta, when she realizes the true identity of Oedipus. See section 10/52a24.

[51]May refer to the fact that emulating or visualizing body

can feel the suffering and passion of the persons. The storming forth seems more real if handled by someone who is agitated, and rage more real if handled by someone angry. This means that poetry is for those who have a gift for this or who have an emotional nature. The first can shape their emotions to those of the person; the second get carried away by their story.

When it comes to the story, whether a legend is adapted or it is constructed from scratch, the poet should begin with a general outline, **[1455b]** then sort out the episodes and elaborate the details.

The outline for *Iphigenia* would be something like this: A young girl is sacrificed and mysteriously disappears. She is transported to a place where strangers are sacrificed to a goddess, and the girl is appointed to be priestess of this goddess. Later her brother arrives. The fact that he was ordered to go there by an oracle and why he decides to do so is outside the plot. When he comes he is captured, and when he is about to be sacrificed, he reveals who he is. The recognition can happen like in the version by Euripides, (10) or in the one by Polyidus, who lets Orestes exclaim: 'So not only my sister, but I too was doomed to be sacrificed,' and this remark saves him.

With the outline in place and names assigned to the persons, it remains to sort out the episodes. We must see how they are relevant to the action. In the case of Orestes, for example, you have the

---

language will also evoke the corresponding emotions.

madness that led to his capture and the cleansing ritual that cured it and saved them.

In the drama, the episodes are short. In the epic poem they give length to the narrative. The plot of the *Odyssey* can be recounted quickly. A man is away for many years, his homecoming blocked by Poseidon. Meanwhile, his home falls into a pity state. [20] Suitors waste his fortune and plot against his son. Finally, after much strain, he returns. He forms some alliances, attacks the suitors, and survives himself while they are killed. This is the core of the plot. The rest is episodes.

18 (55b24) – Tying and Untying

Every tragedy has tying and untying[52]. Incidents outside and often some inside the plot make up the tying.[53] The rest is the untying.

By the tying, I mean all that extends from the beginning of the back story to the point where an arc towards a better or worse situation is set up.

---

[52]Often translated as complication and resolution, which obscures the real meaning and hides the important concept of the knot. Aristotle has the characters untying a knot rather than fighting an antagonist because he finds conflicts revolving around a mistake more inherently tragic than conflicts between good and bad.

[53]Implying that most of the knot is tied in the back story, or that someone is tying it in the background, outside the plot, while the plot follows the attempt to untie. Some tragedies, like Oedipus, start the action right away. Others, like Iphigenia among the Taurians, have an introduction where the knot is explained directly to the audience rather than being shown through emulation. Tying "inside the plot" refer to this and other ways of setting up before the untying action starts.

The untying runs from the beginning of the arc to the end. Thus, in Theodectes' *Lynceus*, (30) the tying consists of the back story and the seizure of the child, while the untying extends from the accusation of murder to the end.

There are four kinds of tragedy, corresponding to the number of parts[54]. The twisted, wholly based on reversal and recognition. Those of traumatic circumstance, for example, tragedies about Ajax[55] and Ixion. Those of character[56], such as Women of Phthia and Peleus. **[1456a]** And fourth, stage

---

[54]This mysterious reference has puzzled scholars as there is no mention of four parts anywhere in the *Poetics* (Lucas, 1968). The placement just after the division of tragedy into tying and untying and together with the four kinds is significant (Schmitt, 2008). If one reverse engineers from the four kinds, the parts appear to be *persons* with *character*, a *knot* with *traumatic circumstances*, an untying *action* with *recognitions and reversals*, and the *mimetic form* of the stage *show*. This corresponds with the division of dance into action, character, circumstance, and performance in *Poetics* 1 (Janko, 1987).

[55]In Ajax the stakes are set high. Violence, slavery, battle. The threats are more important than the execution of them.

[56]Meaning that the personalities of the characters are active causes in the causal chain. Character is revealed through moral choice, but also through other actions that must be explained with reference to personality. If speech and action always spring logically from the situation alone, the tragedy does not have character.

shows[57], like Daughters of Phorcys, Prometheus[58], and those set in Hades.

The poet should try to combine all four, or failing that, as many as possible, prioritizing the most important—more so in the face of the caviling criticism of today. Before there were good poets specializing in one kind, but now the critics expect all to excel in many.

When judging tragedies, it is best to compare the plots. They are equal if the knot (*ploke*) and the untying are the same. Many weave well and

---

[57]The manuscript is corrupt, with at least some letters missing. Those left can look like "show," but many interpret them as simple, with reference to chapter 24 where Aristotle says the epic poems have the same forms as the tragedy and mentions simple before twisted (Sachs, 2005). However, a simple arc cannot carry a plot like surprises, threats of violence, or moral dilemmas. In chapter 14 Aristotle has argued that the stage show can. So from a technical perspective it makes most sense that this is the fourth. Janko (1987) reasons in a similar vein, reaching the same conclusion. This makes it possible to combine all four forms as well, like Aristotle advices. (Simple and twisted arcs are mutually exclusive.) An epic poem cannot, of course, have a stage show, but it has its own mimetic means and way that can be a source of pleasure. They are more suited to be the main element of a short form than an epic poem, though, and Aristotle has in Poetics 13 and probably 14 shown a tendency to leave out cases that are purely hypothetical. In chapter 24 Aristotle seems to remind us of the two types of arcs (simple and twisted) that can be combined with two types of story problems (threats of violence and moral dilemmas), in preparation of the discussion of the Odyssey and Iliad that follows.

[58]In *Prometheus Bound* the immortal *Prometheus*, who gave fire to humankind, is chained to a stone and a spike is hammered through his chest. This pitiable sight stays on stage the whole performance.

(10) untie badly, but both arts should be mastered.

The poet should remember what I have said several times, and not make a tragedy of an epic structure, meaning one that has more than one plot[59]. For instance, try to make a tragedy of the entire *Iliad*. Due to the length of the epic poem, each part will get the right magnitude. In a drama, the result does not answer to the poet's expectations. We have seen this with poets who have dramatized the whole story of the *Sack of Troy*, instead of a part, like Euripides. Or with those who have taken the whole tale of Niobe, and not a piece of her story, like Aeschylus. The plays have either failed completely or experienced little success in competition. Even Agathon experienced his only failure when trying this.

With reversals and single incidents[60], (20) however, the poets can, with astonishing impact, evoke the sympathy and tragic emotions they aim for. This is achieved when a clever villain, like Sisyphus, is outwitted. Or when someone brave but unjust is defeated. Such an unlikely victory is probable, as Agathon puts it, in that 'it is probable that many improbable things would happen.'

The chorus should be treated as one of the actors. It should be integrated into the whole and

---

[59]A plot is the emulation of an action, and Aristotle has said many times that the tragedy should emulate a single action.

[60]Plots with a single action, as opposed to the epic structures with many plots discussed above. Single/simple (*haplos*) plot and action are already used with a different meaning in *Poetics* 10, which explains the odd word choice.

be part of the action, following the example not of Euripides but of Sophocles. With recent poets, the choral songs have little to do with the piece at hand. They could fit into any tragedy; they are just choral interludes. (30) The practice was first begun by Agathon. But what is the difference between injecting such choral interludes and transferring a speech or a whole episode from one play to another?

19 (56a33) – Reason

As the other elements of tragedy have already been discussed, the parts left to speak of are language and reason.

As for reason, I refer to the *Rhetorics*, where this subject belongs. Everything that should be produced by speech falls under reason. This includes proof and refutation, appeals to emotions **[1456b]** such as pity, fear, and anger, and establishing magnitude[61] or the opposite.

The same principles come into play for dramatic incidents when the goal is to evoke pity, fear, urgency or belief. The difference is that the incidents should speak for themselves, without verbal exposition, while the effects of the speech should be produced by the speaker and his words. What is the point of speaking if the thoughts are revealed without uttering them?

When it comes to language, one may examine the forms of speech. (10) This belongs to the study

---

[61]This use of *megethos* as metaphor for *importance* confirms that the stakes are part of the magnitude.

of intonation and to those concerning themselves with this. Examples are what a command, prayer, statement, threat, question, answer, and so on, is.

Criticism directed at poetic works for the right or wrong use of these should not be taken seriously. Who would agree with Protagoras when he criticizes the beginning of Homer's Iliad: "Sing, goddess, of the wrath"? This is giving a command when making a prayer, he says, as telling someone to do or not do something is a command.

But this belongs to another art than poetry, so we put the investigation of it aside.

20 (56b20) – The Parts of Language

Language has the following parts: phonemes, syllables, particles, conjunctions, noun-or-adjectives, verbs, inflections, and utterances.

The phoneme is an indivisible sound. But not all such sounds are phonemes, only those that can be linked to form longer sounds. Even animal sounds are indivisible, but I would not call them phonemes. Of the phonemes, there are three kinds: vowels, semi-vowels, and consonants. A vowel is produced without contact between the parts of the mouth. Semi-vowels, like *s* and *r*, are produced with contact. Consonants, (30) like *g* and *d*, do not have sound in themselves but become audible when linked to a vowel.

Different phonemes are produced by changing the shape of the mouth, the position of contact, the aspiration, the length, and the pitch. A detailed examination of this belongs to the study of meter.

A syllable is a non-descriptive, linked sound, composed of a consonant and a vowel. *Gr* is a syllable, and so is *gra*. The investigation of these distinctions belongs to the study of meter as well.

A particle is a non-descriptive[62] sound, **[1457a]** like *men*, *êtoi*, and *de*, that neither detracts from or contributes to the descriptiveness of an utterance and which (according to Greek grammar) should not be placed at the beginning of it. Or it may be a non-descriptive sound, like *amphi* (around) or *peri* (concerning), that in combination with descriptive sounds, becomes descriptive of something else. A conjunction, like *or*, *because*, or *but*, is a non-descriptive sound which clarifies the beginning, (10) division, or end of a sentence.[63]

A noun-or-adjective is a descriptive[64], linked sound that does not specify a time. As with names, no part is descriptive by itself. In *Theodorus* (divine gift) we do not think of *dorus* (gift) as having a descriptive function.

A verb is a descriptive, linked sound that specifies time. As with the noun-or-adjective, no part is descriptive by itself. *Man* and *white* do not say anything about *when*, but *he walks* and *he has walked*

---

[62]Really *asemos*, non-signifying. Applies to sounds that do not evoke a mental image by itself. Meaningless, modifying, and structural words are all *asemos*.

[63]Following Janko (1987). The Greek text is messed up.

[64]*Semantike* is usually translated as significant or meaningful. Aristotle seems to include only words associated with a meaning that can be visualized, like nouns, adjectives, and verbs.

indicate the present or the past.

Both noun-and-adjectives and verbs have inflections. (20) These indicate relations like *of* or *to*; whether there is one or many, as with *man* or *men*; and the form, such as whether it is a question or a command. 'Gone?' and 'go!' are examples of such verbal inflections.

An utterance is a descriptive, linked sound, where at least some part is descriptive by itself. Not every utterance has both a noun and a verb. The verb may be dropped, like in: "The definition of human." But there is always a descriptive, as "Cleon" is in "Cleon walks".

An utterance can form a unity in two ways, by describing one thing or through linking. The Iliad is (30) one through linking, "the definition of man" by being about one thing.

21 (56b31) – Metaphor

A word can be single, like *ge* (earth), meaning it does not link descriptive parts together. It can be double, meaning that it has one descriptive and one non-descriptive part, although these functions are not maintained in the new word, or that it has two descriptive parts. In the same way, it may be triple, quadruple, and so on, as is the case in Massilian names like *Hermokaikoxanthos*.

[1457b] Words are either common, exotic, metaphorical, ornamental, new, lengthened, shortened, or altered.

By common, I mean words that are frequently

used in a place. By exotic I mean words that are used elsewhere. Clearly, a word that is exotic in one place can be common in another. *Sigunon* (spear) is common on Cyprus, even if we regard it as exotic.

A metaphor is the use of a descriptive that belongs in one context, transferred to another. Either from class (*genos*) to instance (*eidos*), from instance to class, from instance to instance, or by analogy. (10)

An example of class to instance is: "Here my ship rests." The class *resting* includes the instance of *being anchored*. An example of instance to class is: "Odysseus has done ten thousand great deeds." *Ten thousand* is an instance of *many* and is used instead of that word. An example of instance to instance is: "Draining his life with a bronze blade", and "Cutting the water with the bronze bowl." Here *arusai* (drain), is used for *tamein* (cleave), and *tamein* for *arusai*, both being instances of taking away.

A metaphor by analogy is when the second relates to the first as the fourth to the third. Then the poet may put the fourth in place of the second and the second in place of the fourth.

Sometimes, the descriptive that (20) the replaced term relates to is included. The wine bowl relates to Dionysus as the shield to Ares, so you can say that the wine bowl is the shield of Dionysus and that the shield is the wine bowl of Ares. Old age relates to life as the evening to the day, so the evening may be called "the old age of the day", and old age the "evening of life", or, with Empedocles, "the sunset of life".

In some cases, there is no word for one of the things in the analogy, but still this kind of metaphor can be used. For example, to scatter seeds is called sowing, but we do not have a term for the way in which the sun spreads its rays. Still, since the sun spreads its light in the same way that one who sows scatters seed, it has been said that "the sun sows its divine (30) light".

This kind of metaphor may be used in another way as well. After replacing it with another term, one can remove properties from it. For example, by calling a shield not "the wine bowl of Ares", but "the wineless bowl of Ares".

A new word is one that has not been used before, but which is coined by the poet. *Sprouters* for antlers and *prayerist* for priest seem to be such new words.

Lengthening is when a word contains a vowel that is longer than in the common form of the word, **[1458a]** or when an extra syllable is inserted. Shortening is when some part of the word is removed. Examples of lengthening are *poleôs* for *poleôs* (of the city), and *Pêlêiadeô* for *Pêleidou* (son of Peleus). Shortenings are for example *kri* (*krithe*), *dô* (*dôma*), and *ops* (*opsis*), as in *mia ginetai amfoterôn ops* (both eyes see the same things).

There is an alteration when a part of a word is kept and something new is added, like in *dexiteron kata mazon* (in the rightmost breast), with *dexiteron* instead of *dexion* (right).

Of the nouns, some are masculine, some feminine, and some neuter. Masculine nouns are those ending in *n*, *r*, and *s* and (10) letters coupled with *s*: *ps* (psi) and *x* (ksi). Feminine nouns are those ending in vowels that are always long, like *ê* (eta) and *ô* (omega), and *a* when it is long. We see that the number of letters that masculine and feminine nouns end in are the same, since *ps* and *x* are coupled with *s*. No nouns end in a consonant or short vowel. There are three ending in *i*, namely *meli* (honey), *kommi* (gum), and *peperi* (pepper). Five end in U, *astu* (city), *gonu* (knee), *doru* (spear), *sinapu* (mustard), and *pôu* (herd). Nouns that are neither masculine nor feminine end in these two vowels, plus *n* and *s*.

22 (58a17) – Elevated Style

Speech should be clear without being bland.

It is clearest when it uses only common words, but (20) then it is bland. The poetry of Cleophon and Sthenelus demonstrate this.

Speech that uses unfamiliar words is elevated above the ordinary. By unfamiliar, I mean exotic, metaphorical, lengthened, and anything uncommon.

But a poem that uses only such words is either a riddle or gibberish. A riddle if it is made up of metaphors, gibberish if it is made up of exotic words. Riddles point to something by saying something impossible. This cannot be done with bland phrases, but it can by using metaphors, like when referring to medical fire cupping by saying: "I saw him fire weld (30) the bronze to the man". A poem with only exotic terms becomes gibberish.

Thus, a mix is required. The unfamiliar—exotic words, metaphors, ornaments, and the other elements listed—ensures that the poem does not become ordinary and bland. The common ensures clarity.

[1458b] Lengthening, shortening and alteration of words are among the more effective means for making speech both clear and unordinary. The deviation from the common form makes it unordinary, the shared stem makes it clear.

So those who, like old Euclides, criticize and ridicule this, are wrong. To show that it would be easy to be a poet if you could lengthen syllables at whim, he made fun of Homer with these lampoons: "Epicharên eidon Marathônade (10) badisdonta" (Epichares I saw to Marathon walking), and "ouk an geramenos ton ekeinou elleboron" (not mixing for him hellebore).

An excessive use of such techniques is, of course, comical, they must be used with moderation. Metaphors, exotic words, and similar forms of speech, used without moderation, have the same comical effect as when ridicule is intended.

The difference lengthening makes may be seen if we put ordinary words into epic poetry. If we take an exotic word, metaphor, or similar, and replace it with with a common word, it becomes obvious.

Aeschylus and Euripides used the same iambic line, but by replacing (20) a single ordinary word with an exotic one, Euripides made the verse beautiful instead of bland. In Philoctetes Aeschylus has: "the infected wound eats the flesh of my foot". Euripides replaced *eats* with *devours*.

Consider if we changed the unfamiliar words in: "I am today a lousy creature, frail and loathsome", with common, so it said: (30) "I am today a small man, weak and ugly", and compare "setting down a wretched hassock and a skimpy table" with "setting down a simple hassock and a small table", and "the howl of the headlands" with "the noise of the headlands".

Ariphirades ridiculed the tragedians for putting things noone would actually say into speeches, like "domatôn apo" instead of "apo dômatôn", "sethen" instead of "egô de nin", **[1459a]** "Achilleôs peri" instead of "peri Achilleôs", and so on. But these phrases elevate the speech by not being common. Arisphrades failed to understand this.

It is important to be able to use these techniques when they are called for. This goes for double and exotic words, but by far the most important is the metaphor. This alone cannot be taught, it is a gift. Good metaphors require an eye for resemblances.

When it comes to kinds of words, doubles are suited for the dithyramb, exotic for epic poetry, and metaphors for iambic verse. (10) In epic poetry, all the techniques work. In iambic verse, which resembles natural speech, words known from com-

106

mon speech work best, specifically the ordinary, metaphorical, and ornamental.

This is enough on tragedy and on the emulation that is acted out.

23 (59a17) – Epic Poetry

[1459a17] Poetic emulation in narrated verse should have a plot that is constructed in the same way as that of the tragedy. It should emulate a single, whole action, (20) with a beginning, middles[65] and an end[66], be composed to evoke the pleasures that belong to the genre, and the parts should make up an organic whole.

Its structure should not be like that used in history, which by necessity does not portray a single action, but a single period and everything that happened to one or more persons within it, however unrelated these events might be. The sea battle at Salamis and the battle against the Carthaginians in Sicily took place at the same time but did not contribute towards the same end. In the same way, events that follow each other will not always contribute towards a single end. Still, this is how most poets compose their poems. (30)

As stated before, Homer excels in this. He did

---

[65]Plural, as epic poems, as opposed to tragedies, can have parallel plot lines. Each causal chain is one middle.

[66]Here, Aristotle uses *telos* for end instead of *teleute*, which he used in chapter 7. *Telos* can mean intention or aim as well as conclusion or outcome, and Aristotle uses the word in both senses in the rest of this chapter. (Andersen, 2008). A complete action should probably have both aim and conclusion.

not make a poem about the whole Trojan War, even though it has a beginning and an end. The plot would probably have become too large to be easily taken in as a whole. If he had tried to keep it to a reasonable size, it would have become too complex because of the variety. As it is, he has taken one part and diversified the poem by including episodes depicting a variety of situations, such as the catalog of ships.

Other poets choose one hero, a single period or an action with many parts. **[1459b]** The author of *Cypria* and the *Little Iliad* did this. As a result, the *Iliad* and the *Odyssey* give material to one tragedy, or at most two, while the *Cypria* has material for many, and the *Little Iliad* for more than eight; *Judgements of Arms*, *Philoctetes*, *Neoptolemus*, *Eurypylus*, *Vagabondage*, *Laconian Women*, *Sack of Troy*, *Embarkation*, *Sinon*, and *Trojan Women*.

24 (59b7) − Epic Length and Simultaneous Events

Epic poetry has the same types as tragedy, it can have a simple or twisted action, be of character or circumstance.[67] (10) The elements are the same, with exceptions for song and stage show, and it has reversals, recognitions, and circumstance.

---

[67]The list corresponds to action, character, and circumstance. A fourth element is mimetic form. For poetry this means language and reason, which both of Homer's epic poems excel in, as stated below. See also the four parts of tragedy in *Poetics* 18 and of dance in *Poetics* 1.

The reasoning[68] and language should have artistic merit.

In all these respects, Homer is our earliest model and the only one we need. The *Iliad* has a simple action and traumatic circumstances. The *Odyssey* has a twisted action with many recognitions, and situations that reveal character. The language and reasoning of both are unsurpassed.

Epic poetry differs from tragedy in length and meter. When it comes to length, we have already discussed what is adequate. It should be possible to take in both the beginning and the end in a single view. [20] This would be satisfied if the epics were shortened to around the length of the three tragedies usually seen together in a festival sitting. But when it comes to an increased magnitude, epic poetry has an advantage. The tragedy cannot emulate several plotlines happening at the same time. It must confine itself to the one that is acted out on stage.[69] Due to its narrative form, the epic poem can portray simultaneous events. These, when relevant to the action, add length and variety to the poem. This gives the epic poem a special advantage, both when it comes to having a greater scope, [30] and for sustaining interest through variation. Monotony leads to boredom, and this is a challenge for the tragedy.

---

[68]The grouping of reasoning with language indicates that Aristotle sees it as part of the mimetic form. This makes sense as speech is often garnished and rhetorical (Poetics 19).

[69]This is why Aristotle says the tragedy has a singular middle, while the epic poem has plural middles.

The heroic meter has proven itself by withstanding the test of time. If a narrative poem was composed in any other meter today, it would feel wrong. Of all meters, the heroic is the most serene and dignified, and the one that best lends itself to unusual words and metaphors, which is another feature that is specific to narrative emulation.

On the other hand, the iambic trimeter and trochaic tetrameter are energetic meters, with the latter being associated with dance and the former suggesting action. **[1460a]** It would be even more strange to mix meters, as Chaeremon did. Because of this, no one has ever composed a poem of epic length in anything but heroic verse. As indicated, the natural meter has revealed itself to the poets.

Homer deserves praise for many things, but above all for being the only poet who understands his own part. The poet should speak as little as possible in his own voice, as it is not this that makes him an emulator. Other poets speak in their own voice throughout and emulate rarely. (10) Homer, after a few introductory words, brings on a man, woman, or other persons, none lacking in character, each with a personality of their own.

A tragedy should have surprises. But the improbable, which is the most common source of surprises, is more forgivable in epic poetry because the spectators do not see the action. The passage with the pursuit of Hector would look ridiculous on stage, but in the epic poem, the absurdity goes unnoticed. The unexpected is enjoyable, as one can infer from the fact that everyone who tells a story adds a twist of their own, knowing that the listeners like it.

It is Homer who has shown other poets how to correctly lie. (20) The secret is a false inference. If the first implies the second, people think that the second implies the first, but this is false. So, when lying about the first, if one shows that the second is true, the other will be convinced that the first is also true. There is an example of this in the bath scene of the Odyssey.

The impossible that seems plausible should be preferred to the possible that seems implausible. The story should have no implausible parts, above all not inside the plot. If they cannot be avoided, they should be placed outside the plot, (30) like Oedipus not learning how Laius died. Not within, like the messenger's account of the Pythian games in *Electra*, or like the man who goes all the way from Tegea to Mysia without saying anything in *Mysians*. The objection that the plot would be ruined otherwise is ridiculous. Such a plot should not be constructed in the first place.

But even the implausible can be handled more or less skillfully.[70] Take the absurdity found in the *Odyssey* when Odysseus is left on the shore of Ithaca. In the hands of a lesser poet, it could have been intolerable. **[1460b]** As it is, Homer uses his other skills to disguise it.

The language should be most garnished in quiet

---

[70]Following Halliwell (1987).

111

parts that do not reveal character or contain reasoning, as character and reasoning are obscured by excessive garnish.

25 (60b6) – Countering Objections

In the following, we will discuss objections that are raised, how to counter them, and their number and kinds.

As poetry is mimetic, like painting and some other arts, it must emulate one of three; (10) things as they were or are, things as they are said or believed to be, or things as they ought to be. This is narrated in language using unusual terms, metaphors and many modifications used by poets.

Correct does not mean the same in poetry and in civic life any more than it does in poetry and other arts. Poetry has two kinds of problems; central and peripheral. If the poet chose to emulate something but emulated it badly because of lack of ability, the problem is in the art. But if there is an inaccuracy in the chosen motive, if he emulated a horse as putting forth both right legs at the same time, or introduced a medical inaccuracy, for example, (20) or made any other error belonging to another art, the problem is peripheral. This should be kept in mind when addressing the objections.

First, some that concern the art. If something impossible is depicted, there is an error, but it is justified if the aim of the art, as discussed, is reached with more impact because of it. One example of this is the pursuit of Hector. If the aim could be reached

112

better, or at least not worse, without the error, it is not justified, since errors, as far as possible, should be avoided. One should also ask $_{(30)}$ whether the error is central or peripheral. That a painter does not know that hinds have no horns is less serious than the inartistic imitation of it.

Further, if anyone criticizes the poem for not being true, one could counter that it portrays things as they ought to be. Sophocles said he portrayed people as they ought to be, while Euripides portrayed them as they are. If the poem does neither, one could say that things are portrayed as they are said to be, like in the stories about gods. Perhaps they are neither good nor real, but non-existent like Xenophanes thought, but still, people say they are.

[1461a] Other things may be portrayed not as they ought to be, but as they were, like in "the spears stood upright on their butt-ends". This was the custom at that time, as it is among the Illyrians now.

When judging whether someone's speech or action is good or not, one should not only look at what was said or done. One should also look at the person saying or doing it, to whom, when, in what way, to what purpose, and whether it was to improve the situation or to stop it from getting worse[71].

Some objections may be countered by examining

---

[71]This last one is interesting for setting up positive or negative arcs, and reversals. Besides when using the *hamartia* plot, the arc is negative when the hero is on the defensive, and the villain is winning.

the language. (10) By the unusual word in "first against the *oureis*", perhaps Homer does not mean *mules*, but *guards*. Regarding Dolon "who was evil in form", Homer may not mean that he was deformed, but that his face was ugly, as the Cretans call someone good-looking *well-formed*. By "mix the wine purer", he may not mean *stronger*, as in for getting drunk, but *faster*.

Sometimes, an expression is metaphorical, as in "all gods and men slept through the night", while at the same time, "he turned towards the Trojan plain and marveled at the sound of flutes and pipes". *All* is used here as a metaphor for *many*, as *all* is associated with *a lot*. In the verse "she *alone* is denied a plunge", *alone* is a metaphor, (20) as we call the best known the only one.

Pronunciation was the key when Hippias of Thasos solved "but grant that he gains his prayer", and "part rotted in rain".

Objections may be solved by punctuation, as in Empedocles's "suddenly mortal things were born that before learned mortal ways, and things unmixed formerly mixed".

Others can be solved by ambiguity. In "more of the night passed", *more* is ambiguous.

Some can be solved by the use of idioms. Diluted wine is called *wine*. Homer speaks of a "greave of new-forged tin". We call ironworkers bronze-smiths. (30) Ganymede is said "to pour the wine to Zeus," though the gods do not drink wine. The last may also be viewed as a metaphor.

If a word seemingly introduces a contradiction, we should consider the meanings that are possible in the context. For instance, in "there the bronze spear was stopped", we should consider the ways in which a spear could be stopped.

When interpreting we should do the opposite of what Glaucon warns about. He says that some have preconceived assumptions, suppose them correct and start passing judgment. If anything contradicts their own views, they criticize the poet as if he meant what they think he meant.[72] **[1461b]** The question about Icarius has been treated this way. The critics think he was from Sparta, and find it odd that Telemachus did not meet his grandfather when he went there. But perhaps the Cephallenian version is true. They claim that Odysseus found his wife among them and that her father was Icadius, not Icarius. Most likely the objection is founded on a mistake.

Generally, the impossible should be justified with reference to the artistic effect, (10) or to portray things as they ought to be or are said to be. With respect to the artistic effect, a plausible impossibility is preferable to something implausible that is possible. And perhaps the people Zeuxis painted are not possible, but then he chose to make them better. Art should improve on the model. To justify the unlikely, we refer to what is said to be. In addition, the unlikely is not always unlikely, in the sense that it is likely that things contrary to

---

[72]This applies to much commentary on the Poetics itself.

what is likely might happen.

Contradictions should be treated like refutations of arguments. One should examine whether the same thing is meant, relating to the same and in the same sense. The objection should be countered by reference to what the poet says and what an intelligent person would make of it[73].

The impossible and the depraved are rightly criticized (20) when there is no need for introducing them. Examples are the unlikely arrival of Aegeus in *Medea* by Euripides and the badness of Menelaus in *Orestes*.

Altogether, there are five sources of objections. Things are criticized for being impossible, illogical, stupid[74], contradictory, or inartistic. They should be countered in the twelve ways discussed.

26 (61b26) – The Higher Art

One may ask whether epic or tragic emulation is higher.

If less vulgar is better and the less vulgar is that which appeals to a better audience, it is clear that those who emulate everything are vulgar. Believing

---

[73]Probably Aristotle's point is that one should credit the writer with good sense when trying to understand what he meant. Except, of course, when the writer obviously has no sense, which is why he falls back on a phrase that covers both cases.

[74]As in: "Why would the character do something that stupid?" "Morally harmful" is the usual translation, but Elsa Bouchard (2010) argues that it should be interpreted as harmful to the character's own interest. "Stupid" is used in that sense.

that the spectators will not understand anything (30) that is not made explicit, they gesture a lot. Think of the bad flute players who whirl around when they emulate a discus or those who drag the leader of the chorus around when they play *Scylla*.

The tragedy is said to suffer from this kind of problem. There is an analogy in the attitude that some older actors nurtured towards their successors. Mynniscus called Callippides a monkey because he moved so much, and Pindarus was criticized for the same reason. **[1462a]** Tragedy relates to epic poetry like younger actors to older. We are told that epic poetry appeals to a cultivated audience which does not need the gestures. The tragedy appeals to a simpler one, and this makes it the more vulgar, and the lower of the two.

But, first, this objection is not relevant to the poetic art, only to that of performance. Gestures may just as well be overdone in epic recitation, as Sosistratus did, or when singing, as the Opuntian Mnasitheus did.

Next, not all movement can be condemned, or we would have to condemn all dance. Only that of bad performances, like the one of Callippides when he, as are some actors of our own day, was criticized for feminine affectation[75] in female roles. (10)

And, tragedy may, like epic poetry, achieve its effect without movement. It can touch us even when read. So, if the tragedy is better in other

---

[75]What is really meant is unclear, but it is clear that he was criticized for how he depicted female roles.

117

respects, the objection is not relevant.

The tragedy has all the elements of the epic. It may even use its meter. In addition, it has music and stage show, which produce vivid pleasures. It has an impact when read as well as when performed. **[1462b]** It achieves its effect inside tighter boundaries, and a concentrated experience is more pleasurable than one that is spread over a long time. Consider, for example, what would happen to the impact of Sophocles's *Oedipus* if it was given the length of the *Iliad*.

Epic emulation has less unity, as is proven by the fact that an epic poem can supply material for several tragedies. A plot with strict unity would either have to be told concisely, making the poem seem short, or with epic length, and seem watered out. By less unified I mean that it contains several actions. The *Iliad* and the *Odyssey* contain many parts that would have magnitude even if standing alone, (10) although these poems are as well composed as an epic poem could be.

So, if tragedy is better than epic poetry in all this, and it better fulfills the purpose of evoking the pleasures that belong to the art, it is obvious that the tragedy is better than epic poetry at achieving its end.

This is enough on tragedy and epic poetry, their nature and kinds, the parts, their number and the differences between them, what makes them work or not, and on objections and how to counter them.

Cited Sources

If nothing else is stated, references are to the rendering of the translator or to the footnote that accompanies the place in the text.

Andersen, Øivind (Trans.), & Aristoteles. (2008). *Poetikk*. Oslo:Vidarforlaget.

Bouchard, Elsa. (2010). The Meaning of *blaberon* in the Poetics. In *Greek, Roman, and Byzantine Studies* 50 (309–336).

Belfiore, Elsiabeth S. (1992). *Tragic Pleasures: Aristotle on Plot and Emotion*. New Jersey:Princeton University Press.

Berg, Stein (Trans.), Clay, Diskin (Trans.), & Sophocles. (1988). *Oedipus the King (Greek Tragedy in New Translations)*. New York:Oxford University Press. [Ebook]. Retrieved from http://a.co/3fLaWVv

Butcher, S.H. (Trans.), & Aristotle. (1895). The Poetics of Aristotle, London:Macmillan.

Bywater, Ingram. (Trans.), & Aristotle. (1898). The Poetics.

Bywater, Ingram. (Trans.), & Aristotle. (1909). Peri poietikes. Retrieved from https://archive.org/details/peripoietikesont00arisuoft

Else, Gerald F. (1957). *Aristotle's Poetics: The Argument*. Cambrigde:Harvard University Press

Halliwell, Stephen. (1986). *Aristotle's Poetics*. London:Duckworth.

Halliwell, Stephen, & Aristotle. (1987). *The Poetics of Aristotle*. London:Duckworth.

Heath, Malcolm. (2017). *Aristotle on the best kind of tragic plot: re-reading Poetics 13-14*, in R. Polansky and W. Wians (ed.), Reading Aristotle: Exposition and Argument. Leiden:Brill. Retrieved from https://leeds.academia.edu/MalcolmHeath

Howland, Jacob A. (1995). Aristotle on Tragedy: Rediscovering the Poetics. *Interpretation: A Journal of Political Philosophy*, Volume 22(3), 359-405, Retrieved from https://utulsa.academia.edu/JacobHowland

Hubbard, Margaret (Trans.), & Aristotle. (1972). Poetics. In Russel, D.A. & Winterbottom M. (Eds.), *Ancient Literary Criticism* (85-131). Oxford:Oxford University Press.

Janko, Richard (Trans.), & Aristotle. (1987). Poetics. In *Poetics: Bk 1*, Indianapolis:Hackett Publishing Company. [Ebook]. Retrieved from http://a.co/8GuEDOp

Lanouette, Jennine. (1999). *A History of Three-Act Structure*. screentakes.com. Retrieved from http://bit.ly/history-three-act

Lucas, D. W., Aristotle (1968). Aristotle Poetics. Clarendon:Oxford.

Kenny, Anthony (Trans.), & Aristotle. (2013). Poetics. Oxford University Press. [Ebook]. Retrieved from http://a.co/iOxfjtE

Sachs, Joe (Trans.), & Aristotle. (2006). *Poetics.* Annapolis:Focus Publishing.

Schmitt, Arbogast & Aristoteles. (2008). *Poetik* or *Werke in deutscher Übersetzung, Bd. 5*. Berlin:Akademie-Verlag.

Tarán, Leonardo & Gutas, Dmitri. (2012) *Aristotle Poetics*. Boston:Leiden.

Tracy, Stephen V. (1997). The Structures of the Odyssey i A new companion to Homer (s. 360-379). Leiden:Brill.